# Transforming Relationships through Emotional Evolution

## From Inner Work to Lasting Love

**Nathan Dowling**

# Table of Contents

# Chapter One

# **Introduction**

Human relationships are central to our existence, influencing every aspect of our daily lives. Yet, understanding the complexities behind why we connect, communicate, and sometimes conflict with others remains a challenge for many of us. This book seeks to unravel these intricacies by blending scientific insights with relatable stories and historical references, offering a balanced perspective on the socio-psychological factors that shape our interactions. By grounding our exploration in empirical evidence and real-life scenarios, we aim to make the science of human connections accessible and actionable.

One significant issue is that many people engage in relationships without full awareness or intentionality. Often, interactions become routine, driven by habit rather than conscious choice. This lack of mindfulness can lead to misunderstandings, emotional disconnection, and conflict. For instance, consider a situation where a simple misunderstanding escalates because neither party is fully listening or expressing themselves clearly. Such scenarios highlight the need for conscious relationships—those built on empathy, authenticity, and active participation. By focusing on these elements, individuals can cultivate more meaningful and fulfilling connections.

This chapter will establish the framework and primary objectives of our journey into building better relationships. We will explore the concept of conscious relationships in depth, outlining the principles of awareness, intentionality, and active engagement. Additionally, we will introduce key topics such as emotional intelligence, effective communication, and conflict resolution. Through practical exercises and scientifically-backed strategies, you will gain tools to enhance your interactions with partners, friends, and family. Let's embark on this journey together, ready to transform the way we relate to those around us.

## Purpose and Focus of the Book

In a world where relationships play a crucial role in our daily lives, this book delves into the intricate dynamics of human connections by intertwining scientific insights with relatable stories and historical references. Our primary objective is to provide a comprehensive understanding of how sociopsychological factors influence our interactions, behaviors, and emotions. By blending empirical evidence with real-life illustrations, we aim to bridge the gap between science and everyday experiences.

The foundation of this book lies in exploring the concept of conscious relationships. Conscious relationships are built on awareness, intentionality, and active participation. Rather than engaging in mindless interactions, individuals in conscious relationships strive to understand themselves and their partners. They focus on empathy, authenticity, and mutual respect, which form the bedrock of healthy and fulfilling connections.

Emotional factors play a significant role in shaping our memories and perceptions within relationships. George Akerlof and Robert Shiller's extension of Keynesian 'animal spirits' highlights the impact of socio-psychological, non-economic motivations on macro-economic phenomena (Baddeley, M., 2010). Confidence and storytelling, two critical animal spirits, drive herding behavior through narratives that shape our sense of identity and influence our actions. Understanding these dynamics allows us to navigate relationships more effectively, recognizing the underlying forces that affect our choices and interactions.

Another vital aspect of building strong relationships is practicing mindfulness. Mindfulness involves being present and fully engaged in the moment, without judgment. It helps individuals become more attuned to their thoughts, feelings, and surroundings. By cultivating mindfulness, we can enhance our emotional intelligence and improve our ability to connect with others on a deeper level. Practicing mindfulness in relationships encourages open communication, reduces misunderstandings, and fosters a sense of appreciation and gratitude for one another.

Moreover, exploring the benefits of practicing mindfulness reveals that it can lead to reduced stress, enhanced empathy, and better conflict resolution. When we approach relationships with a mindful attitude, we create an environment where positive interactions can thrive. This, in turn, strengthens the bond between partners, friends, and family members.

In addition to socio-psychological influences, evolutionary biology provides valuable insights into our relationship behaviors. Herding instincts, observed in other animals, have evolutionary advantages in social contexts. These instincts encourage monitoring the actions of others, as they provide social information about resource availability and mating potential (Baddeley, M., 2010). Similarly, humans have evolved tendencies to follow social norms and imitate others, which contribute to the formation of cohesive social groups. Recognizing these ingrained behaviors enables us to harness their positive aspects while mitigating potential drawbacks, such as undue conformity or susceptibility to group pressure.

Storytelling further enhances our understanding of relationships by illustrating how shared narratives shape our identities and foster a sense of belonging. Historical examples, like the solidarity movements of the past, demonstrate the power of collective narratives in uniting people towards common goals. By incorporating storytelling into our relationships, we create shared experiences that strengthen our bonds and deepen our connections.

As we progress through this book, we will explore various strategies for building and maintaining healthy relationships. We will delve into techniques for effective communication, developing emotional intelligence, and resolving conflicts constructively. Practical exercises will be provided to help you implement these strategies in your daily life.

This book emphasizes the importance of personal responsibility in relationships while acknowledging the need for a safety net for those who fall on hard times. By balancing individual freedom with social responsibility, we can create an environment where everyone has the opportunity to thrive. Government policies and corporate practices should reflect this balance, ensuring that economic growth does not come at the expense of human welfare.

Ultimately, our goal is to equip you with the knowledge and tools necessary to build meaningful and lasting relationships. Whether it's with your partner, friends, or family, understanding the sociopsychological and evolutionary factors that influence our interactions will empower you to navigate the complexities of human connections more effectively. We invite you to embark on this journey with an open mind, ready to explore the depths of what it means to relate to others in a conscious, intentional, and meaningful way.

## Engagement and Preview of Key Concepts

Have you ever wondered why we feel the way we do in different relationships? What if understanding the science behind our emotions could transform the way we navigate through our interactions with others? This book aims to uncover these mysteries, offering insights that will help enhance the quality of your connections with partners, friends, and family.

At its core, building strong relationships requires effective communication. How often have you found yourself in a misunderstanding, despite having the best intentions? Chapter after chapter, we'll delve into the art of clear dialogue, backed by empirical evidence, to show how expressing ourselves accurately can bridge gaps and foster mutual understanding. Through practical exercises, you'll learn techniques to articulate your thoughts and emotions more effectively, ensuring that your message is both heard and understood.

Emotional intelligence is another cornerstone of flourishing relationships. Understanding not only your own emotions but also those of others can dramatically shift the way you interact. Imagine being able to read between the lines, recognizing subtle cues that reveal what someone else is truly feeling. We'll explore scientifically-backed strategies for enhancing your emotional intelligence, transforming it into a tool for deeper, more empathetic connections.

Conflicts are inevitable in any relationship, but how we handle them makes all the difference. Are you equipped to resolve disagreements in a way that strengthens rather than weakens your bond? We'll examine various conflict resolution techniques, emphasizing the importance of addressing issues without letting them fester. You'll gain skills to navigate contentious topics calmly, finding resolutions that satisfy everyone involved.

Empathy and trust form the bedrock of deep, lasting connections. Consider a time when someone genuinely understood your perspective—it likely created a sense of closeness and trust. This book offers a roadmap to cultivating empathy and building trust step-by-step. By learning to put yourself in others' shoes, you can foster an environment of mutual respect and support that bolsters every interaction.

Cultural influences play a significant role in shaping our relationships. Different backgrounds can bring diverse perspectives, enriching our connections or causing friction if not well-understood. Through real-life examples and scientific explanations, we'll highlight how to navigate cultural differences gracefully, turning potential barriers into bridges for stronger bonds.

To ensure that these principles aren't just theoretical, each chapter includes practical exercises designed to reinforce what you've learned. These exercises range from simple daily practices to more intensive activities aimed at ingraining new habits. For example, implementing daily rituals to stay connected can be transformative:

- Set aside time each day to check in with your partner or friend.

- Share something positive from your day, fostering a habit of positivity.

- Practice active listening, focusing fully on what the other person is saying without planning your response.

- Engage in a shared activity that you both enjoy, strengthening your bond through common interests.

For long-term strategies for sustained relationship growth, consistency and effort are key:

- Schedule regular "relationship check-ins" where you discuss what's working well and areas for improvement.

- Celebrate milestones together, big or small, to create lasting positive memories.

- Continuously seek new ways to grow together, whether through joint hobbies, travel, or learning opportunities.

- Encourage each other's personal growth, supporting new endeavors and celebrating individual achievements.

Through these guidelines, you'll find that maintaining and growing healthy relationships becomes second nature. As you progress through the book, each section will build upon the last, creating a comprehensive framework for understanding and improving your relationships.

By the end of this journey, you'll have a robust toolkit of knowledge and practices to apply to your daily interactions. Whether it's on the topic of communication, emotional intelligence, conflict resolution, empathy, trust, or cultural differences, you'll be equipped with the insights needed to create and maintain strong, meaningful relationships. So, let's dive in and start transforming the way we connect with each other, one step at a time.

## Practical Value for You

In this chapter, we have established the primary framework and objectives of our book on building relationships. We explored the concept of conscious relationships, emphasizing awareness, intentionality, and active participation. By understanding sociopsychological factors and incorporating mindfulness, we can enhance how we connect with others.

We discussed the influence of emotions, confidence, and storytelling in shaping our interactions and identities. The impact of evolutionary biology and herding instincts provided further insight into our social behaviors. Recognizing these ingrained patterns helps us harness their positive aspects while being mindful of potential drawbacks.

As we navigate through this book, you'll gain tools to improve communication, emotional intelligence, and conflict resolution. Practical exercises will guide you in applying these strategies, fostering deeper and more meaningful connections.

Our current position is clear: by blending scientific insights with real-life illustrations, we aim to bridge the gap between theory and everyday experiences. This approach allows for a comprehensive understanding of the dynamics at play in our relationships.

You may be concerned about balancing individual freedom with social responsibility. It's essential to remember that personal growth and societal well-being are not mutually exclusive. Government policies and corporate practices must reflect this balance, ensuring that economic progress does not come at the expense of human welfare.

Looking at the broader implications, stronger relationships contribute to a more cohesive and empathetic society. By cultivating empathy, authenticity, and mutual respect, we create environments where everyone has the opportunity to thrive.

As we continue this journey together, I encourage you to remain open-minded and curious about the depths of human connections. By delving into the complexities of relationships with intention and awareness, we can transform the way we relate to one another, ultimately enriching our lives and the lives of those around us.

# References

An, U., Han, D., Kim, Y., Park, H. (2022, January). *Emotional Suppression and Psychological WellBeing in Marriage: The Role of Regulatory Focus and Spousal Behavior. International Journal of Environmental Research and Public Health.* None.

Baddeley, M. (2010, January). *Herding, social influence and economic decision-making: sociopsychological and neuroscientific analyses. Philosophical Transactions of the Royal Society B: Biological Sciences.* https://www.ncbi.nlm.nih.gov/pmc/articles/PMC2827453/.

University of West Alabama. (2019, June). *The Science of Emotion: Exploring the Basics of Emotional Psychology | UWA Online. UWA Online.* https://online.uwa.edu/news/emotionalpsychology/.

# Chapter Two

# Understanding the Foundations of

# Relationships

Human relationships are at the core of our existence, shaping who we become and how we navigate the world. The foundation of these connections is built upon myriad psychological and sociological principles that have evolved over time. From the familial bonds we form in childhood to the diverse and complex relationships we engage in as adults, understanding these underlying principles provides a key to unlocking healthier, more fulfilling interactions.

One major shift in relationship dynamics can be observed through historical changes in societal roles. For instance, traditional family structures often assigned rigid gender roles, with men as breadwinners and women as homemakers. These roles were not just personal but deeply influenced by socio-economic conditions and cultural norms. Over time, movements advocating for gender equality have reshaped these roles, allowing for more egalitarian partnerships. Additionally, historical events like the Great Depression and World War II have had profound effects on family dynamics and relationship structures, demonstrating how external factors can redefine interpersonal connections.

In this chapter, you will explore the basic psychological and sociological principles that underpin human relationships. By examining historical perspectives, cultural influences, and the impact of technology, the chapter delves into how each of these elements shapes our interactions. The discussion aims to provide insights into the complexities of human connections, helping you appreciate the intricate web of factors that influence relationships today. Through this understanding, individuals can better navigate their own relationships, fostering deeper and more meaningful connections.

# Investigating historical perspectives on human connections to understand their evolution and impact on present-day relationships.

When we examine the historical evolution of relationships, we see a marked shift from traditional structures to modern ones. Traditional relationships often followed rigid roles, where men were the breadwinners and women managed the home and children. These dynamics were heavily influenced by societal norms and economic necessities at the time. Over the years, these roles have evolved, influenced by various social reforms and movements advocating for gender equality and individual rights.

Societal changes have significantly shaped the nature of human connections. For example, the women's liberation movement in the 1960s led to increased participation of women in the workforce and a shift towards more egalitarian relationships. As societies became more democratic, the emphasis on personal freedom and choice grew stronger, impacting how relationships are formed and maintained. Policies promoting equal rights and opportunities have also played a crucial role in redefining relationship norms.

Historical events have always left a lasting impact on relationship norms. The Great Depression, for instance, saw families returning to cooperative economies within households due to economic hardships. World War II brought about long separations and the need for women to manage households alone, which altered family dynamics and paved the way for more independence among women post-war.

Family structures have been instrumental in defining relationship patterns. In the past, the nuclear family model was the ideal, with extended families living together being common in many cultures. Modern family structures have become more diverse, including single-parent households, blended families, and cohabiting couples. This diversity reflects broader societal acceptance of different family forms and the changing definitions of what constitutes a family (Concordia University, 2020).

Cultural influences deeply affect relationship behaviors and expectations. Cultural backgrounds dictate everything from gender roles to the importance placed on familial duties and obligations. For example, in collectivist cultures, family ties and responsibilities might take precedence over individual desires, whereas, in individualist cultures, personal fulfillment is often prioritized. Common cultural practices such as arranged marriages, communal living, or paternal authority can significantly shape how relationships operate within those cultural contexts. Cultural values like honor, respect, and duty can either bridge gaps or cause conflicts in intercultural relationships.

Intercultural relationships come with both challenges and benefits. Navigating different cultural backgrounds demands openness and adaptability. Here is what you can do to handle the complexities:

- Approach each other's cultural backgrounds with curiosity and respect.

- Communicate openly about differences and establish mutual understanding.

- Be willing to compromise and find common ground.

- Celebrate cultural differences through shared experiences.

Technological advancements have undeniably transformed the landscape of relationships. Social media and digital communication channels have made it easier to connect with people across distances but have also introduced new challenges regarding maintaining relationship quality and authenticity. The immediacy and convenience of virtual interactions sometimes replace deeper, in-person connections, leading to superficial engagement. While technology can enhance connectivity, it often blurs the lines between meaningful relationships and digital acquaintances.

The implications of virtual interactions on real-life relationships are profound. The reliance on digital communication can sometimes lead to misunderstandings or misinterpretations, given the lack of non-verbal cues. Moreover, the constant connectivity can contribute to issues like digital burnout and reduced face-to-face interaction. Despite these challenges, finding strategies to maintain genuine connections is crucial.

To maintain genuine connections in the digital age:

- Prioritize regular in-person interactions whenever possible.

- Set boundaries for screen time to ensure focused, quality time together.

- Use technology mindfully, opting for video calls over text when discussing important matters.

- Engage in shared activities that do not involve screens to strengthen bonds.

Understanding the basic psychological and sociological principles that underpin human relationships involves looking at how history, culture, and technology influence our connections. By examining these factors, we gain insight into the complex web of influences that shape our interactions and relationships. Historical shifts, cultural backgrounds, and technological advances each play pivotal roles in framing how we relate to one another, and understanding these can help us navigate our relationships more effectively. Through this lens, we can appreciate the nuances that make each relationship unique while acknowledging the broader patterns that influence them.

## Exploring the biological underpinnings of social bonding to illuminate the innate aspects of human connections.

The neurobiology of connection is a fascinating area that explores the neurological mechanisms driving human bonding. It's incredible how our brains are wired to connect with others, often without us even realizing it. Neurotransmitters such as oxytocin and dopamine play significant roles in fostering social connections. Oxytocin, often dubbed the "love hormone," promotes feelings of trust and bonding, while dopamine, known for its role in reward and pleasure, enhances the joy we feel when we connect with others. Understanding these chemical processes can illuminate why certain relationships feel so fulfilling.

Attachment styles also significantly impact relationship dynamics. Secure attachment styles foster healthy, balanced connections marked by mutual respect and support. In contrast, insecure attachment styles, which may arise from early relationship experiences with caregivers, can lead to patterns of anxiety, avoidance, or both, affecting how individuals interact in their adult relationships (Vrtička et al., 2012). Recognizing your attachment style can be the first step toward fostering healthier interactions.

Brain development further influences interpersonal relationships. The brain's capacity for empathy and emotional regulation grows over time, shaped by both genetic and environmental factors. These developmental stages highlight the critical period during childhood when forming secure bonds can have lasting impacts on future relationships. It underscores the necessity of nurturing environments that promote healthy emotional growth.

From an evolutionary perspective, our social behaviors are deeply rooted in survival strategies. Historically, forming bonds increased our ancestors' chances of survival and reproduction. Mate selection, influenced by evolutionary psychology, often mirrors these age-old priorities. People tend to seek partners who exhibit signs of health, stability, and the ability to provide resources, traits that historically would contribute to the survival of offspring.

Physiological responses also play a critical role in relational experiences. Emotional regulation directly correlates with relationship quality. Effective

21

emotional regulation can enhance communication and reduce conflict, leading to more rewarding relationships. Here is what you can do to achieve effective emotional regulation:

- Identify your emotions and triggers.

- Practice mindfulness to stay present and manage stress.

- Develop healthy coping mechanisms like deep breathing or physical activity.

- Communicate your feelings clearly and constructively.

Stress significantly affects interpersonal interactions. When stressed, people might misinterpret signals or react defensively, which can strain relationships. It's essential to recognize stressors and develop strategies to manage them, ensuring they don't spill over into personal interactions. Here is what you can do to minimize stress in relationships:

- Acknowledge and discuss stress openly with your partner.

- Prioritize self-care routines to maintain emotional balance.

- Encourage supportive dialogues that focus on mutual understanding.

- Seek professional help if stress overwhelms your relationship dynamics.

Physical touch is another vital component in fostering emotional connections. Simple gestures like holding hands, hugging, or a pat on the back release oxytocin, enhancing feelings of closeness and security. Touch provides reassurance and communicates care beyond words, strengthening relational bonds. To incorporate more physical touch in your relationship:

- Offer a comforting hug or hold hands during challenging conversations.

- Express affection through small, consistent acts of touch.

- Be mindful of your partner's comfort level with physical touch.

- Use touch to show empathy and support during stressful times.

In conclusion, exploring the basic psychological and sociological principles that underpin human relationships reveals the deep-seated mechanisms that guide our interactions. From the neurobiology of connection to evolutionary perspectives and physiological responses, understanding these elements provides invaluable insights into improving our relationships. By acknowledging the roles of neurotransmitters, attachment styles, brain development, evolutionary history, emotional regulation, stress management, and physical touch, we can foster deeper, more meaningful connections with those around us.

# Analyzing sociopsychological theories of relationships to provide a framework for understanding relational dynamics.

Social Exchange Theory explores how individuals weigh the costs and rewards of their relationships, much like an economic transaction. At its core, this theory suggests that people aim to maximize benefits and minimize costs in their interactions. When the perceived rewards of a relationship outweigh the costs, satisfaction generally follows (Tulane University, 2018). This cost-benefit analysis varies greatly from person to person based on their unique comparison levels, which are shaped by past experiences and personal expectations.

In relationships, equity plays a crucial role. Equity refers to a fair distribution of costs and rewards between partners. When one party feels overburdened or underappreciated compared to their partner, it can lead to dissatisfaction. To maintain harmony, both parties should strive for a balance where contributions are reciprocated adequately.

Attachment Theory sheds light on how early bonding experiences influence adult relationships. Secure attachment, often formed through consistent and responsive caregiving, fosters trust and healthy interdependence in adulthood. However, insecure attachment styles—such as anxious or avoidant—can create challenges in forming stable and satisfying relationships. Early relational patterns establish a template for future interactions, impacting how individuals approach intimacy and resolve conflicts.

To address the role of attachment in conflict resolution and emotional intimacy:

- Acknowledge your attachment style and its influence on your behavior.

- Practice open communication to express needs and concerns without fear of judgment.

- Develop patience and empathy towards your partner's attachment-related behaviors.

- Seek professional guidance if attachment issues persistently disrupt the relationship.

Moving on to Social Learning Theory, this concept explains how we acquire relational behaviors through observation and imitation. Observational learning plays a substantial part in how we navigate relationships, especially during formative years. Watching parents, siblings, or peers interact sets a script for our own behaviors. For instance, witnessing reinforcement or punishment in others' interactions teaches us what is acceptable or unacceptable in our own.

Reinforcement and punishment further shape our interactions. Positive reinforcement—such as praise or affection—encourages the continuation of desirable behaviors, while negative reinforcement or punishment can deter unwanted actions. It's vital to recognize the impact of these elements when analyzing why certain relational patterns exist and how they can be modified for better outcomes.

Exploring modeling and imitation reveals how behaviors seen in influential figures are replicated in our relationships. If you observe respectful and understanding exchanges growing up, you're more likely to emulate those behaviors in your partnerships. Conversely, consistently witnessing conflict or disrespect might lead to similar conduct in your relationships.

For fostering emotional intimacy:

- Build emotional safety by ensuring your partner feels secure and valued.

- Share vulnerabilities and encourage your partner to do the same.

- Engage in active listening, showing genuine interest in your partner's thoughts and feelings.

- Employ non-verbal communication, including physical touch, to strengthen emotional bonds.

Understanding Social Exchange Theory, Attachment Theory, and Social Learning Theory gives us a comprehensive framework for navigating relationships. By examining costs and rewards, recognizing the influence of early attachment, and considering the effects of learned behaviors, individuals can better understand and improve their relational dynamics. The emphasis lies in balancing economic growth with human welfare, ensuring that personal responsibility and a safety net coexist to support those in challenging times.

# Exploring the role of early life experiences in relationship development to highlight the origins of relational patterns.

Family Dynamics and Relationship Patterns

Understanding family dynamics is crucial in exploring how upbringing influences relationship choices. Our families-of-origin, where we first learn about relationships, significantly impact our future interactions. The way we handle conflict, express love, and seek intimacy often mirrors these early lessons.

Intergenerational transmission of relational behaviors is another key aspect. We inherit not just physical traits but also patterns of behavior and interaction. Observing our parents' relationships guides our own. If they resolved conflicts with respect and communication, we are likely to adopt similar strategies. Conversely, witnessing negative patterns can lead to adopting unhealthy behaviors unless consciously addressed.

One significant factor in shaping adult attitudes towards intimacy and trust is childhood experiences. Here's what you can do to achieve healthier relationship dynamics:

- Reflect on your past to identify patterns or behaviors rooted in childhood.

- Seek therapy if needed to address deep-seated issues.

- Build self-awareness and understand how past experiences influence present actions.

- Practice mindfulness and conscious decision making in relationships.

Trauma and Relationship Resilience

Early-life trauma impacts relationship resilience and coping mechanisms. Traumatic experiences during formative years can profoundly affect one's attachment styles. Research indicates that individuals with secure attachments generally experience healthier relationships, while those with insecure attachments often struggle with trust and intimacy (Cassioli et al., 2022). Recognizing and addressing these patterns is crucial for relationship resilience.

Healing from past wounds is pivotal for fostering healthier relationships. Here's what you can do:

- Engage in therapies like cognitive-behavioral therapy (CBT) or eye movement desensitization and reprocessing (EMDR).

- Develop a support network of friends and family.

- Practice self-care and stress-management techniques.

- Cultivate positive interactions and gradually build trust.

Self-awareness plays a critical role in breaking intergenerational cycles of dysfunction. Here's how to enhance it:

- Keep a journal to document thoughts and feelings.

- Reflect on your actions and their underlying motivations.

- Seek feedback from trusted individuals.

- Participate in personal development workshops or courses.

Parental Modeling and Socialization

Parental modeling and socialization deeply influence relationship skills. Children observe their parents and mimic their behavior. Healthy parental relationships teach effective communication, empathy, and conflict resolution. A parent's approach to love and intimacy sets a template for the child's future relationships.

Communication patterns within families also get transmitted across generations. Families that practice open, honest dialogue facilitate better understanding and strong bonds. On the contrary, families with poor communication often leave children ill-equipped for healthy interactions.

Conscious parenting is essential in fostering positive relationship behaviors. To achieve this:

- Demonstrate healthy relationships through actions.

- Encourage open communication and active listening.

- Model empathy and respect in all interactions.

- Provide a stable and loving environment for children to thrive.

Understanding how early life experiences shape relational patterns equips us with the knowledge to cultivate healthier dynamics. By reflecting on our upbringing, addressing traumas, and engaging in conscious parenting, we can foster relationships grounded in trust, respect, and mutual understanding.

## You will gain a comprehensive understanding of how various factors influence the foundations of human relationships.

In this chapter, we explored the roots of human relationships through a psychological and sociological lens. We examined historical shifts from traditional to modern relationship structures, detailing how societal changes like the women's liberation movement and economic events like the Great Depression shaped our current understanding of familial and romantic bonds. Cultural influences were highlighted, illustrating how different backgrounds impact relational behaviors and expectations. The emergence of diverse family structures and the effects of technology on human connections were also discussed.

We looked at how cultural context affects relationships, whether in collectivist or individualist societies, and the role of history in shaping these dynamics. Recognizing the importance of historical context allows us to better understand the evolution of relational norms and appreciate the diversity in modern family configurations. Additionally, technology's dual role was considered—while it facilitates global connectivity, it also presents challenges in maintaining authentic interactions.

Understanding these foundational principles helps us navigate the complexities of our current social environment. By acknowledging how historical and cultural forces intersect with personal experiences, we gain a nuanced view of what shapes our relationships today. This perspective encourages us to approach relationships with greater empathy and adaptability, recognizing that each connection is influenced by a unique blend of factors.

As you reflect on their relationships, they should be mindful of the broader socio-historical contexts while also considering the influence of personal and cultural background. By doing so, individuals can foster healthier, more fulfilling connections. The implications of these insights stretch beyond personal interactions; they contribute to a more empathetic and interconnected society.

Ultimately, understanding the basic psychological and sociological principles underpinning human relationships fosters deeper connections. As we continue to explore these themes, we should remain open to the evolving nature of relationships, adapting and growing along with the changing landscape of human interaction.

## References


Blumenthal, S., Young, L. (2023, June). *The Neurobiology of Love and Pair Bonding from Human and Animal Perspectives. Biology.* https://www.mdpi.com/2079-7737/12/6/844.

Cassioli, E., Castellini, G., Gironi, V., Innocenti, M., Ricca, V., Rossi, E., Sanfilippo, G., Scami, I., Tarchi, L. (2022, March). *Attachment Style and Childhood Traumatic Experiences Moderate the Impact of Initial and Prolonged COVID-19 Pandemic: Mental Health Longitudinal Trajectories in a Sample of Italian Women. International Journal of Mental Health and Addiction.* None.

Concordia University. (2020, July). *The Evolution of American Family Structure. CSP Online.* https://online.csp.edu/resources/article/the-evolution-ofamerican-family-structure/.

Kapfhammer, H., Lahousen, T., Unterrainer, H. (2019, December). *Psychobiology of attachment and trauma—some general remarks from a clinical perspective. Frontiers in Psychiatry.* https://www.ncbi.nlm.nih.gov/pmc/articles/PMC6920243/.

Nickerson, C. (2023, October). *Social Exchange Theory - Simply Psychology. www.simplypsychology.org.* https://www.simplypsychology.org/what-is-social-exchangetheory.html.

Tulane University. (2018, April). *What Is Social Exchange Theory?. Tulane University School of Social Work.* https://socialwork.tulane.edu/blog/social-exchange-theory/.

VanOrman, A. (2016, August). *Understanding the Dynamics of Family Change in the United States.* *PRB.*
https://www.prb.org/resources/understandingthe-dynamics-of-family-change-in-the-unitedstates/.


Vrtička, P., Vuilleumier, P. (2012). *Neuroscience of human social interactions and adult attachment style. Frontiers in Human Neuroscience.* None.

# Chapter Three

# The Role of Communication in Building Strong

# Connections

Strong relationships are built on the foundation of effective communication. The way we convey our thoughts, feelings, and intentions plays a crucial role in how connections are formed and maintained. Whether through spoken words or unspoken gestures, each interaction contributes to the strength and quality of our interactions. Understanding the nuances of communication can significantly enhance our ability to connect with others on a deeper level.

One common challenge in communication is the alignment between verbal and non-verbal cues. Verbal communication consists of the words we speak, which should be clear and direct. However, words alone often aren't enough. Non-verbal communication, such as body language, facial expressions, and tone of voice, can sometimes speak louder than words. For instance, crossed arms may suggest defensiveness, even if the words spoken are agreeable. A mismatch between what we say and how we say it can lead to misunderstandings and weaken relationships. Active listening is another vital aspect that ensures the message received is the message intended. It requires being fully present and engaged in the conversation, reflecting back what has been heard, and asking clarifying questions when necessary.

This chapter will delve into the various facets of communication, exploring both its verbal and nonverbal components. It will provide insights into how these elements interact and contribute to building stronger connections. You will learn practical strategies for aligning their verbal messages with their non-verbal cues to convey their thoughts more effectively. Additionally, the chapter will cover techniques for becoming a more active listener, fostering empathy, and maintaining clarity in communication. By understanding and applying these principles, individuals can enhance their relationships, creating a foundation of trust and mutual understanding.

# Understanding the different facets of communication and how they contribute to relationship building

Understanding the interplay between verbal and nonverbal communication is key to building strong, healthy relationships. Verbal communication involves the words we use to convey our thoughts and messages clearly. On the other hand, non-verbal cues include body language, facial expressions, tone of voice, and even silence. When both forms of communication align, the message is clearer and more likely to be understood as intended.

Non-verbal cues can often speak louder than words. A warm smile or a reassuring touch might communicate comfort and support more effectively than any verbal affirmation. Effective communication isn't just about what we say but how we say it. Our body language, eye contact, and tone of voice can significantly influence how our words are received. For instance, saying "I'm fine" in a monotone voice with crossed arms likely indicates quite the opposite. It's essential to match our verbal and non-verbal signals to avoid misunderstandings.

Aligning these two forms of communication is crucial for clarity and understanding. Here is what you can do to achieve this:

- Pay close attention to your body language when speaking.

- Use gestures that match your words to emphasize your points.

- Maintain appropriate eye contact to show engagement and sincerity.

- Be mindful of your tone of voice; ensure it reflects your true feelings and intentions.

Non-verbal communication plays an important role in expressing emotions and intentions accurately. It helps us convey our true feelings, sometimes even those we aren't completely aware of ourselves. An open posture can indicate acceptance and readiness to listen, while a furrowed brow may suggest concern or confusion. Recognizing these subtle hints can help us respond more empathetically to others.

Active listening is another cornerstone of effective communication that enhances understanding and empathy. Active listening goes beyond hearing words; it involves fully engaging with the speaker and paying attention to their message. This can foster deeper connections by showing genuine interest and respect.

To hone active listening skills, consider these techniques:

- Summarize or paraphrase what the speaker has said to confirm understanding.

- Ask clarifying questions if something is unclear.

- Avoid interrupting; let the speaker finish their thoughts before responding.

- Provide feedback through nodding or short verbal acknowledgments to show you are engaged.

Engaging in empathetic listening means putting yourself in the speaker's shoes, trying to understand their emotions and perspectives without judgment. When someone feels heard and understood, it nurtures trust and strengthens the bond between individuals.

One key takeaway here is the importance of balancing verbal and non-verbal communication. By being attentive to both forms, we can convey our messages more effectively and build stronger connections. Remember that communication is a two-way street—actively listening and responding appropriately can make all the difference in enhancing relationships.

In conclusion, mastering both verbal and non-verbal communication and practicing active listening are essential skills for fostering healthy and meaningful relationships. They allow us to express our thoughts and feelings clearly while also understanding and empathizing with others. By focusing on these aspects, we can create a more harmonious and connected world.

# Addressing common barriers to effective communication and methods to overcome them

Overcoming communication barriers can be a challenge, but it's essential for fostering healthy relationships. Identifying and addressing obstacles that impede clear communication is crucial. Common barriers such as poor listening skills, distractions, preconceived notions, and emotional triggers can significantly hinder effective communication.

To overcome these barriers, consider strategies such as mindfulness, patience, and openness. Mindfulness involves being fully present during conversations, which helps in understanding the nuances of what is being communicated. Patience allows for thoughtful responses rather than reactive ones, which can lead to more meaningful exchanges. Openness involves being receptive to differing viewpoints and feelings, enabling a richer dialogue.

Cultivating self-awareness and empathy is also vital. Self-awareness involves recognizing your own biases and emotions that may affect how you communicate. Empathy allows you to understand the emotions and perspectives of others, reducing misunderstandings and promoting constructive dialogue. By practicing these qualities, you create an environment conducive to open and honest communication.

Expressing emotions effectively is another cornerstone of healthy relationships. When emotions are articulated with clarity, honesty, and sensitivity, they foster emotional intimacy and trust. This means not just saying how you feel but also doing so in a way that respects both your feelings and those of the other person.

Embracing vulnerability is key to deepening emotional bonds. Sharing vulnerabilities requires courage but can significantly enhance connections. When you express yourself authentically, it encourages others to do the same, creating a space for mutual understanding and support. Authentic expression of emotions strengthens the emotional foundation of any relationship.

Here are some practical steps to express feelings healthily and constructively:

- Start by identifying your emotions clearly.

- Use "I" statements to express how you feel without blaming the other person.

- Be specific about what has triggered your emotions.

- Listen actively when others share their emotions.

- Validate the emotions of others, showing that you acknowledge and understand their feelings.

Effective communication isn't limited to spoken words; it encompasses active listening, empathy, and non-verbal cues. Active listening, as highlighted, involves genuinely paying attention to the speaker, acknowledging their message, and responding thoughtfully. It's not just about hearing words but understanding the underlying emotions and contexts. Techniques like maintaining eye contact, nodding, and summarizing what the other person has said show that you are engaged and value their perspective.

Empathy in communication bridges gaps created by differing life experiences and viewpoints. By putting yourself in someone else's shoes, you can better understand their thoughts and feelings, leading to more compassionate interactions. This doesn't mean you have to agree with everything they say, but it shows respect for their viewpoint.

Remember, overcoming communication barriers and expressing emotions effectively requires practice and commitment. By incorporating these strategies into your daily interactions, you can build stronger, more meaningful relationships based on mutual understanding and trust. These efforts not only improve how you connect with others but also enhance the overall quality of your relationships.

## Enhancing communication skills to navigate conflicts and challenges in relationships

Effective communication is often the cornerstone of healthy relationships. This section delves into strategies for conflict resolution and the development of emotional intelligence—two critical components in fostering strong connections.

Conflict resolution requires practical approaches, and effective communication is key. When disagreements arise, employing techniques like active listening is crucial. Listening actively means fully concentrating on what the other person is saying rather than planning your response while they speak. Empathy also plays a significant role; it's about putting yourself in the other person's shoes to better understand their perspective. Respect for each other's viewpoints, even if they differ from your own, helps de-escalate tensions and move toward a compromise.

Here is what you can do to manage disagreements and conflicts through effective communication:

- Address the conflict directly rather than avoiding it. Ignored issues often become larger over time.

- Clarify the issue causing the conflict. Ensure all parties have a mutual understanding of the problem.

- Bring involved parties together to talk. Allow everyone to express their viewpoints in a safe environment.

- Identify solutions that are acceptable to everyone involved. Aim for a win-win outcome where possible.

- Monitor and follow up to ensure the solution is being implemented and working as intended.

Using communication tools like "I" statements and reflective listening also aids in managing conflicts. "I" statements help express feelings without blame, such as saying, "I feel hurt when..." instead of "You always...". Reflective listening involves paraphrasing what the other person has said to confirm understanding and show you're engaged in the conversation. For example, saying, "So what I'm hearing is..." helps ensure both parties are on the same page.

Cultivating emotional intelligence (EI) is another vital aspect of effective communication. Emotional intelligence involves being aware of your emotions and expressing them appropriately. In relationships, this self-awareness translates to understanding what triggers certain emotions in you and why. It allows you to manage these emotions constructively, preventing them from spilling over into conflict unnecessarily.

Guidelines for developing awareness of emotions and enhancing emotional expression include:

- Practice mindfulness to recognize your emotional state before reacting.

- Use journaling as a tool to explore and understand your feelings better.

- Engage in open discussions about emotions with trusted individuals to develop emotional fluency.

- Incorporate relaxation techniques like deep breathing or meditation to maintain emotional balance.

Empathy is a foundational component of EI that facilitates better communication. By understanding and sharing the feelings of another, you create a basis for more harmonious interactions. Strengthening your emotional intelligence, therefore, leads to more empathetic and supportive relationships, where conflicts are less likely to escalate and more likely to be resolved constructively.

Ultimately, effective communication and emotional intelligence form the bedrock of healthy relationships. Through mindful listening, empathetic engagement, and structured conflict resolution strategies, individuals can navigate disagreements in ways that foster deeper understanding and stronger bonds. As we continue to develop these skills, our capacity for maintaining fulfilling and resilient relationships grows exponentially.

# Practicing effective communication to create a foundation of trust and connection in relationships

Fostering trust through communication is essential in building strong relationships. Trust forms the bedrock upon which all other aspects of a relationship rest, whether personal or professional. When we communicate transparently, empathetically, and honestly, we create a safe space for others to be themselves without fear of judgment or deceit. This kind of openness invites reciprocity and nurtures mutual respect.

Here is what you can do in order to achieve this goal:

- Be clear and transparent about your intentions and actions.

- Express empathy by acknowledging and validating the other person's feelings.

- Practice honesty, even when it's uncomfortable, to build a lasting foundation of trust.

Repairing breaches in trust can be challenging but not impossible. Sincere communication, accountability, and a willingness to rebuild are crucial steps in this process. When trust is broken, addressing it directly and with genuine remorse helps to begin the mending process. Accountability means admitting mistakes and taking steps to rectify them, demonstrating a commitment to change. Rebuilding takes time and patience, but consistent effort can restore the trust that was lost.

Here is what you can do in order to achieve this goal:

- Engage in a sincere conversation to address the breach.

- Take responsibility for your actions and apologize genuinely.

- Commit to behavioral changes and follow through consistently.

Deepening emotional connection through communication enriches relationships, fostering intimacy and understanding. Sharing vulnerabilities creates an environment of closeness, where both parties feel seen and valued. Expressing gratitude amplifies positive emotions and reinforces the bond between individuals. Practicing empathy allows us to understand and share the feelings of another, further deepening our connection.

Utilizing communication to deepen emotional bonds involves more than just talking; it requires active listening and meaningful engagement. When we invest time in significant conversations, we learn more about each other's inner worlds, interests, and values. Validating each other's emotions, even if we don't always agree, ensures that both parties feel heard and respected. Through these practices, we cultivate a sense of belonging and togetherness that can withstand the tests of time and adversity.

Cultivating emotional connection through communication not only strengthens the current state of the relationship but also sets a solid foundation for long-term closeness. It's like tending to a garden—consistent care, attention, and nurturing lead to beautiful, flourishing connections. By making conscious efforts to communicate, listen, and empathize, we pave the way for enduring relationships filled with mutual respect and love.

Key takeaways for enhancing relationships through effective communication include understanding the power of transparent and honest dialogue, recognizing the importance of repairing trust with sincerity and accountability, and using communication as a tool to deepen emotional bonds. By integrating these practices into our daily interactions, we stand to build stronger, more resilient relationships grounded in trust and mutual understanding.

## Key takeaways

Throughout this chapter, we have explored the various facets of communication and their significance in building strong, healthy relationships. We started by examining the interplay between verbal and non-verbal communication, emphasizing how both must align to convey messages effectively. A warm smile or a reassuring touch, for instance, often communicates more comfort and support than words alone.

We then delved into the importance of active listening as a fundamental aspect of effective communication. Active listening involves fully engaging with the speaker, summarizing their points, asking clarifying questions, and avoiding interruptions. This not only enhances understanding but also fosters empathy and deeper connections.

Additionally, we discussed common barriers to effective communication, such as poor listening skills, distractions, preconceived notions, and emotional triggers. Overcoming these obstacles requires mindfulness, patience, openness, self-awareness, and empathy. By practicing these qualities, we can create an environment conducive to open and honest dialogue.

Effective communication also plays a critical role in conflict resolution. Addressing conflicts directly, clarifying issues, and seeking mutually acceptable solutions help manage disagreements constructively. Techniques like using "I" statements and reflective listening further aid in navigating conflicts by expressing feelings without blame and confirming understanding.

Cultivating emotional intelligence (EI) is another vital element in successful communication. Being aware of and managing our emotions allows us to express them constructively, preventing unnecessary conflicts. Empathy, a core component of EI, helps bridge gaps created by differing life experiences and viewpoints, leading to more harmonious interactions.

As we continue to develop our communication skills, it's essential to remember that trust forms the foundation of all relationships. Transparent, empathetic, and honest communication builds trust and fosters mutual respect. Repairing breaches in trust requires sincere communication, accountability, and consistent efforts to rebuild.

Ultimately, enhancing our communication skills enables us to create stronger, more meaningful relationships based on mutual understanding and trust. By focusing on clear expression, active listening, empathy, and emotional intelligence, we pave the way for deeper connections and a more harmonious interpersonal dynamic.

As you reflect on this chapter, consider how these strategies can be applied in your relationships. The journey to better communication is ongoing, and each step taken brings us closer to building fulfilling and resilient connections.

# References

Anguera, M., Del Giacco, L., Salcuni, S. (2020, February). *The Action of Verbal and Non-verbal Communication in the Therapeutic Alliance Construction: A Mixed Methods Approach to Assess the Initial Interactions With Depressed Patients. Frontiers in Psychology.* https://www.ncbi.nlm.nih.gov/pmc/articles/PMC7047748/.

Cohn, K. (2017). *Developing Effective Communication Skills. Journal of Oncology Practice.* https://www.ncbi.nlm.nih.gov/pmc/articles/PMC2793758/.

Ellis, V., Ronquillo, Y., Toney-Butler, T. (2023, July). *Conflict Management. National Library of Medicine.* https://www.ncbi.nlm.nih.gov/books/NBK470432/.

Krakoff, S. (2023, November). *The Top 5 Conflict Resolution Strategies for the Workplace. online.champlain.edu.* https://online.champlain.edu/blog/top-conflict-resolutionstrategies.

Kwame, A., Petrucka, P. (2021, September). *A literature-based study of patient-centered care and communication in nurse-patient interactions: Barriers, facilitators, and the way forward. BMC Nursing.* https://bmcnurs.biomedcentral.com/articles/10.1186/s12912-021-00684-2.

# Chapter Four

# Cultivating Emotional Intelligence

motions are the silent architects of our relationships, shaping how we interact with others daily. Understanding emotional intelligence (EQ) can transform not only how we feel about ourselves but also how we connect with those around us. Whether it's an exchange with a colleague or a deep conversation with a loved one, our ability to navigate and manage emotions plays a crucial role in fostering healthy interactions. As life becomes increasingly complex, mastering EQ offers a pathway to creating more fulfilling, harmonious relationships.

A common issue many people face is the difficulty in recognizing and regulating their emotions. For instance, during a heated discussion, it's easy to get overwhelmed by anger or frustration, which can lead to regrettable words or actions. This lack of emotional control often results in misunderstandings and strained relationships. On the other hand, individuals who understand their emotional triggers and responses can mitigate conflicts more effectively. They can take a step back, breathe, and address the situation calmly, paving the way for constructive dialogue instead of destructive arguments.

In this chapter, we will explore the key components of emotional intelligence and their profound impact on relationship dynamics. We'll delve into the essential aspects of self-awareness and self-regulation, explaining how they form the foundation for managing emotions. Additionally, we will examine the roles empathy and social skills play in building strong, meaningful connections. By understanding and practicing these elements, you will not only enhance your personal growth but also improve your ability to communicate and resolve conflicts, ultimately leading to healthier, more rewarding relationships.

## Exploring the components of emotional intelligence and how they contribute to relationship dynamics.

Understanding emotional intelligence is integral to fostering healthy relationships. At its core, emotional intelligence comprises self-awareness, self-regulation, empathy, and social skills. Recognizing and managing emotions enhances effective communication and conflict resolution.

Emotional intelligence begins with recognizing one's own emotions and their impact on interactions. By gaining insight into our feelings, we can better control our responses. This awareness is crucial when navigating disagreements or misunderstandings.

To manage emotions effectively:

- **Take a moment to breathe:** Pause before reacting to regain composure.

- **Reflect on the situation:** Consider why you're feeling a certain way.

- **Adjust your perspective:** Shift focus to understand the other person's viewpoint.

Developing empathy involves seeing the world through another's eyes. It builds a deeper connection and often fosters mutual respect. Empathy demands genuine interest in others' experiences and emotions.

To cultivate empathy:

- **Listen actively:** Pay attention without planning your response.

- **Show understanding:** Acknowledge their feelings and concerns.

- **Ask questions:** Encourage them to share more about their experiences.

Social skills enhance rapport and positive interactions. These skills include effective communication, active listening, and the ability to manage conflicts constructively. Strong social skills help build and maintain relationships by demonstrating respect and consideration for others.

To improve social skills:

- **Communicate clearly:** Express thoughts and feelings openly and respectfully.

- **Practice active listening:** Give full attention and provide feedback.

- **Resolve conflicts calmly:** Address issues directly but sensitively, aiming for a win-win outcome.

In conclusion, mastering these elements of emotional intelligence can significantly enhance relationship quality. By focusing on managing our emotions, developing empathy, and honing social skills, we create a foundation for stronger, more meaningful connections.

# Delving into the importance of self-awareness and self regulation in fostering healthy relationships.

Understanding emotional intelligence and its impact on relationships involves exploring key concepts like self-awareness and self-regulation, which are critical for fostering healthy connections. Cultivating emotional self-awareness is the first step towards understanding oneself better. By becoming attuned to your own emotions, you gain insight into what triggers certain reactions and how these responses manifest in your behaviors. This level of awareness allows you to recognize patterns that might be helpful or harmful in your interactions with others.

To cultivate emotional self-awareness:

- Reflect regularly on your emotional experiences.

- Pay attention to physical cues that might signal an emotional response.

- Keep a journal to document daily emotions and identify patterns over time.

- Seek feedback from trusted friends or mentors about how you express and manage emotions.

Self-regulation, on the other hand, involves managing impulses and reactions to promote more constructive interactions. It's essential for maintaining composure and responding thoughtfully rather than reactively. When we regulate our emotions effectively, we not only improve our communication but also create space for healthier dialogue and conflict resolution.

To enhance self-regulation:

- Practice deep breathing or mindfulness techniques to stay calm under pressure.

- Develop a habit of pausing before reacting, considering the consequences of your actions.

- Engage in activities that reduce stress and increase patience, such as yoga or exercise.

- Reflect on past situations where impulsive reactions led to negative outcomes and consider alternative approaches.

Increasing self-awareness and self-regulation collectively leads to better communication and conflict resolution skills. As you become more aware of your internal states and better at managing them, you can express yourself more clearly and listen more effectively to others. This clarity in communication helps prevent misunderstandings and fosters a culture of respect and empathy within relationships.

Here are practical steps to improve self-awareness and self-regulation for enhancing relationships:

- Regularly set aside time to reflect on your feelings and behavior in recent interactions.

- Notice physical sensations associated with different emotions and learn what they signify.

- Make a conscious effort to think before reacting, especially in emotionally charged situations.

- Engage in practices like meditation or journaling to maintain emotional balance and resilience.

The benefits of these practices are well-documented. Research suggests that individuals who see themselves clearly tend to be more confident, creative, and capable decision-makers. They build stronger relationships and communicate more effectively, leading to increased personal and professional satisfaction (Eurich, T., 2018). Moreover, cultivating self-awareness helps in recognizing one's strengths and areas for improvement, guiding personal and relational growth.

Managing your impulses through self-regulation means less friction and more harmony in relationships. It allows for thoughtful exchanges instead of heated arguments, and it promotes problem-solving over blame. This balanced approach not only strengthens individual connections but also contributes to a more supportive and understanding community overall.

In addition, fostering these skills aids significantly in conflict resolution. By understanding your own emotional landscape, you can approach conflicts with a mindset geared towards resolution rather than escalation. You become better equipped to understand the perspectives of others and find common ground, which is essential for resolving disputes amicably.

To implement these strategies effectively:

- Begin by acknowledging your emotional responses without judgment.

- Utilize coping strategies like taking breaks or walking away momentarily when emotions run high.

- Communicate your feelings and needs clearly and respectfully during discussions.

- Practice active listening to ensure that you understand the other person's point of view completely before responding.

Ultimately, the integration of self-awareness and self regulation into daily life can transform the way we interact with those around us. These skills are not just about managing negative emotions but also about enhancing positive experiences. They help create a foundation of trust and mutual respect, making relationships more fulfilling and resilient against challenges.

By prioritizing human welfare and ensuring that our emotional intelligence is finely tuned, we can navigate our interactions with greater empathy and effectiveness. This balance between understanding ourselves and managing our responses lies at the heart of nurturing meaningful and lasting relationships.

# Discussing the role of empathy and social skills in building strong connections.

Empathy fosters understanding and compassion in relationships. It allows individuals to connect on a deeper level by recognizing and sharing the feelings of others. This mutual understanding builds a foundation of trust, creating an environment where both parties feel valued and respected. Empathy is not just about feeling for someone but also about taking action to support and comfort them.

Social skills are essential tools in any relationship, as they encompass effective communication, active listening, and conflict management. To enhance these skills, consider the following steps:

- Practice attentive listening without interrupting, which shows respect and interest in what the other person is saying.

- Use clear and concise language to express your thoughts and feelings, minimizing misunderstandings.

- Develop non-verbal communication techniques, like maintaining eye contact and open body language, to reinforce your spoken words.

- In disagreements, focus on the issue at hand rather than personal attacks, aiming for a resolution that respects both viewpoints.

Developing social skills involves recognizing the importance of active listening. By truly hearing what the other person is expressing, we validate their experiences and emotions. This strengthens the bond and fosters mutual respect. Additionally, being able to manage conflicts calmly and constructively is crucial. Conflict is inevitable, but how we handle it determines the health of the relationship. Instead of reacting defensively, approach conflicts with the intent to understand and resolve, promoting a cooperative atmosphere.

Empathy and social skills are intertwined. When we empathize with others, we naturally become better communicators and listeners. This dynamic creates emotionally rich interactions, enhancing our connections and deepening our relationships.

Here is what you can do to develop empathy and social skills effectively:

- Make a conscious effort to put yourself in others' shoes and see things from their perspective.

- Engage in regular self-reflection to understand your own emotional responses and how they affect your interactions.

- Seek feedback from trusted friends or mentors on your social interactions and use it constructively to improve.

- Participate in activities that require teamwork and collaboration, as these situations naturally build empathy and social skills.

By nurturing empathy and honing social skills, you cultivate an environment where emotional bonds thrive, and respect becomes a natural outcome. Individuals who excel in these areas tend to create more meaningful and long-lasting relationships. They communicate more effectively, navigate conflicts with ease, and support one another through challenges.

Moreover, empathy enables us to recognize and respond to the needs of those around us, fostering a sense of community and belonging. As we grow more empathetic, we find ourselves becoming more patient, compassionate, and understanding, which are all critical components in sustaining healthy relationships.

Developing these qualities is not an overnight process but requires ongoing commitment and practice. It begins with small, consistent efforts to be more present in our interactions, paying close attention to the verbal and non-verbal cues of those we engage with.

In essence, while empathy brings depth and warmth to relationships, social skills equip us with the practical tools to navigate various social landscapes effectively. The balance of these elements ensures that our relationships are not only strong but also resilient and adaptable to change.

Incorporating these practices into your daily life can transform your interpersonal dynamics, leading to more fulfilling and harmonious connections. The journey towards better relationships through empathy and social skills is a rewarding one, filled with opportunities for personal growth and greater emotional intelligence.

## Exploring strategies for developing emotional resilience to navigate relationship challenges.

Developing Emotional Resilience: Cultivating resilience enables individuals to bounce back from setbacks and conflicts. When we talk about emotional resilience, we're referring to the ability to recover quickly from difficulties. In relationships, this means not letting every argument or misunderstanding lead to a downward spiral. Instead, it's about learning from these experiences and coming back stronger.

Here is what you can do in order to achieve the goal:

- Practice mindfulness techniques to stay grounded during stressful moments.

- Develop a support network of friends or family who can provide perspective and encouragement.

- Reflect on past experiences where you overcame challenges to remind yourself of your capabilities.

- Engage in regular self-care activities to maintain your mental well-being.

Resilience fosters adaptability and growth within relationships. It allows us to be flexible and openminded, making our interactions more dynamic and enriching. By being emotionally resilient, partners can handle changes and challenges in their relationship without feeling overwhelmed or stuck. This adaptability is crucial for long-term relationship success as it encourages continuous growth and mutual understanding between partners.

Building emotional resilience supports effective problem-solving and stress management in interpersonal connections. When faced with conflicts or misunderstandings, emotionally resilient individuals are better equipped to navigate these issues constructively. They can remain calm and focused, which helps in finding mutually beneficial solutions rather than escalating the conflict.

Here is what you can do in order to achieve the goal:

- Adopt a problem-solving mindset by identifying the issue clearly and thinking of possible solutions.

- Communicate openly and honestly with your partner about what's bothering you instead of bottling up emotions.

- Take breaks if discussions get too heated, giving both parties time to cool down and think rationally.

- Consider seeking professional help if recurring issues are too challenging to manage on your own.

By fostering emotional resilience, individuals become more adept at handling the ups and downs of relationships. This not only strengthens the bond between partners but also enhances individual wellbeing. Knowing how to bounce back from setbacks and manage stress effectively creates a more harmonious and supportive environment for everyone involved.

Emotional resilience isn't just about bouncing back; it's also about growing through adversity. When we face challenges, whether in our personal lives or relationships, those experiences shape us. They teach us valuable lessons about ourselves and others, building a deeper understanding and empathy that enriches our connections. For example, when a couple goes through a tough time together, such as a financial crisis or health scare, their ability to pull through can strengthen their bond. They learn to rely on each other's strengths and develop a more profound sense of trust and partnership.

In addition to personal growth, resilience improves communication. When we are resilient, we tend to communicate more effectively because we are less likely to be hampered by negative emotions like fear, anger, or frustration. This clarity of mind and emotional stability allows for more productive conversations, where both parties feel heard and understood.

Stress management is another critical benefit of emotional resilience. Stress can wreak havoc on relationships, leading to miscommunication, irritability, and even resentment. By developing resilience, we equip ourselves with tools to manage stress better, reducing its negative impact on our interactions with others. Techniques such as deep breathing exercises, regular physical activity, and maintaining a positive outlook can be instrumental in managing stress levels.

It's worth noting that resilience can also prevent burnout. In relationships, especially those involving caregiving or dealing with chronic issues, burnout can be a real threat. Being resilient means having the stamina and emotional strength to keep going, even when things get tough. It involves setting boundaries, asking for help when needed, and taking time to recharge.

Ultimately, fostering emotional resilience leads to healthier, more fulfilling relationships. It encourages a positive cycle where overcoming one challenge makes us better prepared for the next, creating a stable and supportive foundation for lasting connections. By investing in our emotional resilience, we not only improve our relationships but also enhance our overall quality of life.

## Key takeaways

Throughout this chapter, we have delved into the components of emotional intelligence and their impact on relationships. By exploring self-awareness, self-regulation, empathy, and social skills, we have gained valuable insight into how these elements contribute to healthy interpersonal dynamics.

We began by highlighting the importance of recognizing our own emotions and understanding their impact on interactions. Developing self-awareness allows us to identify emotional triggers and manage our responses more effectively. This foundational step is crucial for navigating disagreements and misunderstandings with greater composure.

Self-regulation, a key aspect of emotional intelligence, involves controlling our impulses and reactions. By pausing before reacting and considering the consequences of our actions, we promote constructive communication and conflict resolution. Engaging in activities that reduce stress and foster patience further enhances our ability to regulate emotions in challenging situations.

Empathy emerged as another vital component in building strong connections. By seeing the world through another's eyes, we deepen our understanding and forge stronger bonds based on mutual respect. Active listening and genuine interest in others' experiences help us cultivate empathy, creating an environment where everyone feels valued and heard.

Social skills were also identified as essential tools for fostering positive interactions. Effective communication, active listening, and conflict management are all integral to maintaining healthy relationships. By expressing ourselves clearly and respectfully, we minimize misunderstandings and demonstrate consideration for others.

While mastering these elements of emotional intelligence requires ongoing effort, the benefits extend far beyond individual relationships. On a broader scale, these skills contribute to a more empathetic and supportive community. As individuals become more adept at managing their emotions and connecting with others, they foster environments of trust and cooperation.

As you consider these insights and practices, reflect on their potential to transform your relationships. The journey to enhancing emotional intelligence is continuous and ever-evolving. By prioritizing self-awareness, self-regulation, empathy, and social skills, you lay the groundwork for meaningful and lasting connections. Embrace this journey with openness, and let it enrich both your personal and communal interactions.

# References


Aguilar-Parra, J., Fernández-Campoy, J., López-Liria, R., Mercader, I., Morales-Gázquez, M., Rocamora, P., Sanchez-Sanchez, E., Trigueros, R. (2020, January). *Relationship between Emotional Intelligence, Social Skills and Peer Harassment. A Study with High School Students. International Journal of Environmental Research and Public Health.* None.

Cavaness, K., Fleshman, J., Picchioni, A. (2020). *Linking Emotional Intelligence to Successful Health Care Leadership: The Big Five Model of Personality.*

*Clinics in Colon and Rectal Surgery.* https://www.ncbi.nlm.nih.gov/pmc/articles/PMC7329378/.

Eurich, T. (2018, January). *What self-awareness really is (and how to cultivate it). Harvard Business Review.* https://hbr.org/2018/01/what-selfawareness-really-is-and-how-to-cultivate-it.

Landry, L. (2019, April). *Why emotional intelligence is important in leadership. Harvard Business School Online.* https://online.hbs.edu/blog/post/emotionalintelligence-in-leadership.

Pervez, N. (2022, December). *The study of mindfulness as an intervening factor for enhanced psychological well-being in building the level of resilience. figshare.com.* https://figshare.com/collections/

The study of mindfulness as an intervening fact or for enhanced psychological wellbeing in building the level of resilience/ 6354431.


Ringwald, W., Wright, A. (2020, December). *The Affiliative Role of Empathy in Everyday Interpersonal Interactions. European Journal of Personality.* https://doi.org/10.1002%2Fper.2286.


Sutton, A. (2016, November). *Measuring the effects of self-awareness: Construction of the SelfAwareness Outcomes Questionnaire. Europe's Journal of Psychology.* https:// www.ncbi.nlm.nih.gov/pmc/articles/PMC5114878/.

# Chapter Five

# Navigating Conflicts Constructively

onflicts are an inevitable part of relationships, whether they occur with a partner, friend, or family member. These moments of disagreement can be challenging but also offer opportunities for growth and understanding. Rather than viewing conflicts as purely negative, we can approach them as chances to improve communication and strengthen our bonds with one another.

Common sources of conflict often include miscommunication, differing expectations, and unresolved issues from the past. For instance, a simple misunderstanding in a conversation can escalate if not addressed promptly, leading to feelings of frustration and resentment. Differing expectations about roles and responsibilities within a relationship can create tension when these expectations are not aligned. Additionally, unresolved issues tend to resurface during stressful times, magnifying current disagreements and making them more difficult to manage.

This chapter will explore various strategies for managing and resolving conflicts healthily. It will delve into recognizing personal and relational patterns that contribute to conflicts, effective techniques for de-escalating tensions, and adapting conflict resolution styles to suit different situations. By focusing on clear communication, empathy, and mutual respect, you will learn how to navigate conflicts constructively, turning potential points of friction into opportunities for deeper connection and harmony.

# Understanding common sources of conflict and how to address them constructively

Conflict is an inevitable part of any relationship, be it with a partner, friend, or family member. Understanding the common sources of conflict can help us navigate and resolve disagreements in a healthy manner. Often, conflicts arise from miscommunication, differing expectations, and unresolved issues. By recognizing these triggers, we can address potential conflicts before they escalate. It's crucial to identify personal and relational patterns that contribute to conflicts, as this insight can offer valuable clues on how to manage them effectively.

Recognizing triggers involves being mindful of situations where miscommunication might occur. Open channels of communication are vital. Ensure that both parties clearly understand the messages exchanged. Misunderstandings often lead to feelings of frustration and resentment, which can easily spiral into larger conflicts. By preemptively clarifying intentions and expectations, you minimize the chances of miscommunication leading to disagreement.

It's also important to acknowledge that everyone has unique expectations based on their values, experiences, and beliefs. When these expectations clash, it can create tension. Take time to discuss and align expectations openly and honestly. This process of alignment helps create a shared understanding, reducing the likelihood of conflict stemming from unmet or misunderstood expectations.

Addressing unresolved issues is another key aspect. Lingering problems can resurface under stress, amplifying current disagreements. Commit to resolving past issues and forgive genuinely. This not only prevents the past from burdening the present but also strengthens trust and understanding in the relationship.

When conflicts do arise, different conflict resolution styles come into play. Understanding these styles and their appropriate applications can make a significant difference in outcomes. There are various approaches to conflict resolution: compromising, collaborating, accommodating, competing, and avoiding. Each style has its strengths and weaknesses, depending on the nature of the conflict and the dynamics of the relationship.

Compromising involves each party giving up something to reach a mutually acceptable solution. This can be effective in situations where both concerns are equally important. Collaborating seeks a win-win solution by addressing the needs and concerns of all involved, fostering mutual respect and partnership. Accommodating places one's needs aside for the benefit of the other person, useful when maintaining harmony is more important than being right. Competing focuses on asserting one's viewpoint at the expense of another's, appropriate in situations requiring quick, decisive action. Avoiding entails sidestepping the conflict altogether, suitable for trivial issues not worth the energy.

Adapting your conflict resolution style to the circumstances can lead to better outcomes. Assess the context and relationship, then choose a style that suits the situation best. Flexibility and a willingness to switch tactics can prevent conflicts from becoming entrenched.

During conflicts, tensions can run high, and emotions can overpower rational thinking. Techniques for deescalating tensions are essential in such scenarios. Practical methods like breathing exercises, active listening, and taking breaks can help in calming heightened emotions. Breathing deeply and slowly can reduce physical symptoms of stress, making it easier to think clearly. Active listening ensures that the other party feels heard and understood, which can diffuse anger and resentment. Taking a break during a heated argument can provide the time needed to cool off and approach the issue with a clearer mind.

Additionally, learning to express thoughts and feelings in a non-confrontational way is crucial. Using "I" statements rather than accusatory "you" statements prevents the other party from feeling attacked, creating a safer space for open dialogue. For example, saying, "I feel hurt when..." rather than, "You always...".

Building compromise and consensus is fundamental in conflict resolution. Finding common ground and mutually beneficial solutions requires patience, empathy, and active listening. Empathy allows you to see things from the other person's perspective, understanding their feelings and needs. This shared understanding fosters trust and openness, making it easier to reach compromises.

Valuing the relationship over individual positions can facilitate healthier resolutions. It means prioritizing the connection over winning an argument. When both parties value the relationship, they're more likely to work collaboratively toward solutions that benefit everyone. Remember, the goal is not to win but to resolve.

In summary, managing and resolving conflicts healthily involves recognizing triggers, choosing appropriate conflict resolution styles, de-escalating tensions, and building compromise and consensus. By focusing on clear communication, empathy, and mutual respect, it's possible to navigate conflicts constructively, strengthening relationships and fostering long-term harmony.

# Enhancing communication skills in conflict situations for effective resolution—Active listening in conflicts

In any conflict, active listening is indispensable. It's a crucial step towards understanding the root causes of disagreements. By genuinely focusing on what the other person is saying, one can uncover the underlying issues that might otherwise be overlooked. Active listening involves not just hearing but truly comprehending and acknowledging the concerns and emotions being expressed.

Practicing reflective listening to demonstrate understanding and validate the other person's perspective

Reflective listening goes hand in hand with active listening. It entails summarizing or paraphrasing what the other person has said to show that you understand their point of view. This technique not only demonstrates empathy but also validates the other person's feelings and perspectives.

Here is what you can do in order to achieve the goal:

- Pay close attention to the speaker without interruptions.

- Summarize or reflect back what you heard.

- Confirm if your reflection is accurate and ask for clarification if needed.

- Show empathy through your tone and choice of words.

Using open-ended questions to clarify concerns and promote dialogue in conflict situations

Open-ended questions are powerful tools in conflict resolution. They encourage deeper dialogue by allowing individuals to express themselves more fully, rather than limiting their responses to simple yes or no answers. This promotes a more constructive and insightful conversation.

Here is what you can do in order to achieve the goal:

- Use questions that start with "how," "what," or "why" to invite elaboration.

- Avoid leading questions that may bias the response.

- Encourage the other person to explain their thoughts and feelings in detail.

- Listen actively to the responses and follow up with further relevant questions.

Expressing emotions constructively: Teaching the art of expressing feelings in a respectful and nonaccusatory manner

Expressing emotions constructively during conflicts is essential for maintaining respect and preventing escalation. It's about communicating how you feel without blaming or accusing the other party. This approach helps in addressing the issue at hand rather than getting sidetracked by personal attacks.

Here is what you can do in order to achieve the goal:

- Use "I" statements to express your feelings (e.g., "I feel upset when...").

- Avoid making accusatory statements like "You always..." or "You never...".

- Focus on describing your emotions and their impact on you.

- Seek to address specific behaviors rather than attacking character traits.

Encouraging assertive communication while respecting boundaries and emotions

Assertive communication is about being honest and direct while still respecting others' feelings and boundaries. It strikes a balance between passivity and aggression, ensuring that one's own needs are expressed without disrespecting the other party.

Here is what you can do in order to achieve the goal:

- Clearly state your needs and concerns without minimizing them.

- Respect the other person's right to have their own needs and perspectives.

- Use firm yet calm language to convey your message.

- Maintain a level-headed demeanor even if emotions run high.

Providing techniques for communicating needs and emotions without escalating conflicts

Effective communication techniques help convey needs and emotions clearly while keeping conflicts from escalating. These techniques foster understanding and mutual respect, paving the way for resolution.

Here is what you can do in order to achieve the goal:

- Practice deep breathing to stay calm before speaking.

- Choose your words carefully to avoid triggering defensive reactions.

- Maintain an even tone and avoid raising your voice.

- Focus on finding solutions rather than dwelling on problems.

Managing non-verbal cues

Non-verbal cues play a significant role in conflict resolution. Body language, facial expressions, and tone of voice can all influence how messages are perceived. Being mindful of these cues helps in ensuring that the intended message is effectively communicated.

Understanding how non-verbal communication can affect the perception of messages during conflicts

Non-verbal communication significantly impacts how messages are received during conflicts.

Misinterpretations of body language or tone can exacerbate tensions. Therefore, being aware of and controlling non-verbal cues is crucial.

Here is what you can do in order to achieve the goal:

- Maintain eye contact to convey attentiveness.
- Use open body language to show you are approachable and willing to engage.
- Be conscious of facial expressions that might convey unintended emotions.
- Monitor your tone of voice to ensure it matches your intended message.

Practicing mindfulness to regulate non-verbal cues and promote positive communication

Mindfulness can be an effective technique in managing non-verbal cues. By staying present and aware, one can better control their body language and tone, promoting a more positive and constructive dialogue.

Here is what you can do in order to achieve the goal:

- Take a moment to breathe deeply and center yourself before engaging in conflict discussions.
- Pay attention to your physical sensations and adjust your posture and gestures accordingly.
- Stay focused on the present moment and listen fully to the other person.

- Reflect on your own non-verbal signals and make adjustments to align them with your verbal messages.

Key takeaways: You will learn to listen actively, express emotions effectively, and be mindful of nonverbal cues to improve communication and resolve conflicts constructively. Successful conflict resolution hinges on these skills, fostering healthier and more productive relationships.

# Developing skills for deescalating conflicts and finding common ground

Conflict is inevitable, but the way we manage it can make all the difference. By incorporating assertiveness and empathy into negotiation strategies, we can navigate conflicts more effectively. To start, it's crucial to separate the people from the problem. By focusing on the issue at hand rather than personal attributes, we prevent emotions from clouding our judgment. This approach ensures that discussions remain productive.

When negotiating, it's important to focus on interests, not positions. Rather than arguing over fixed demands, we should explore underlying needs and motivations. Understanding what truly matters to each party paves the way for mutual agreements. This principle is central to principled negotiation, which emphasizes fair and objective criteria over opinion-based arguments (principled negotiation. PON - Program on Negotiation at Harvard Law School., n.d.).

Brainstorming a variety of options for mutual gain is another key strategy. Before settling on a solution, we should take time to generate multiple possibilities. This increases the likelihood of finding an agreement that satisfies everyone involved.

Using these techniques, let's practice negotiation through examples and scenarios. Imagine a workplace setting where two colleagues disagree about a project timeline. Instead of sticking rigidly to their own schedules, they could discuss why those timelines are important. Perhaps one colleague needs the project done quickly for an upcoming meeting, while the other requires more time for thorough research. By understanding these underlying interests, they might find a compromise that respects both needs.

In another scenario, consider a family dispute over holiday plans. Each family member may have a different vision for how to spend the holidays. By facilitating a conversation where everyone shares their interests – be it spending time together, relaxation, or visiting extended family – the group can brainstorm ways to incorporate elements of each person's desires into a cohesive plan.

Forgiveness plays a vital role in resolving conflicts and rebuilding relationships. Holding onto grievances only prolongs emotional pain. Forgiveness doesn't mean forgetting or excusing the past; it means letting go of resentment. This act can be profoundly healing for both individuals and the relationship.

Understanding the healing power of forgiveness involves recognizing that it benefits the forgiver as much as the forgiven. Letting go of anger and bitterness can reduce stress and improve mental health. It opens the door to reconciliation, allowing relationships to move forward positively.

Offering methods for initiating reconciliation involves taking concrete steps to rebuild trust. Here are some actions you can take:

- Show genuine remorse if you've wronged someone. Acknowledge your mistakes honestly.

- Make amends where possible, demonstrating your commitment to change.

- Engage in open and honest communication, creating spaces for both parties to express feelings and concerns.

- Be patient and give time for wounds to heal, as rebuilding trust is a gradual process.

These steps are essential for mending relationships and fostering long-term trust.

You will acquire invaluable skills through understanding these principles. They will learn how to navigate negotiations with both assertiveness and empathy, striving for win-win solutions using the principles of principled negotiation. Additionally, they'll recognize the importance of forgiveness in conflict resolution, seeing how it helps not just individuals but also strengthens relationships. Moreover, by practicing these methods, you will understand how to initiate reconciliation and rebuild trust after conflicts.

Applying evidence-driven strategies allows us to tackle conflicts comprehensively and humanely. Balancing assertiveness with empathy, focusing on interests rather than positions, and embracing forgiveness and reconciliation will empower us to transform conflicts into opportunities for growth and connection.

# Cultivating empathy and understanding for effective conflict resolution

Empathy in conflict resolution is a cornerstone for understanding others' perspectives during disagreements. It's more than just putting oneself in another's shoes; it's about genuinely connecting with their experiences and emotions. Empathy does not imply agreement but recognizes the validity of differing viewpoints. By fostering empathy, we can better navigate conflicts, acknowledging that each party brings unique backgrounds and emotions to the table.

Practicing empathic communication involves actively listening to acknowledge emotions and needs when conflicts arise. This can be done by allowing space for the other person to express themselves without interruption, showing genuine interest through nonverbal cues like nodding, and reflecting back what you've heard. For example, if someone feels unheard at work, responding with "It sounds like you're feeling overlooked in meetings" can validate their experience.

Here is what you can do in order to achieve empathic communication:

- Focus on the speaker, maintaining eye contact, and using body language to show engagement.

- Avoid interrupting or planning your response while the other person is speaking.

- Summarize what the other person has said to ensure understanding and validate their feelings.

- Use open-ended questions to explore their perspectives further and show that you value their contributions.

Demonstrating empathy through active listening and validating the other person's experiences is crucial. Active listening goes beyond hearing words; it involves interpreting emotions and underlying messages. Validating another's experiences might include statements like, "I can see why this situation would be frustrating for you." This acknowledgment helps build trust and opens pathways for collaborative problem-solving.

Building emotional intelligence in conflicts requires enhancing one's awareness and regulation of emotions. Emotional intelligence (EI) entails recognizing one's own emotions and understanding how they influence behavior and interactions. During conflicts, being emotionally intelligent means staying calm rather than reacting impulsively, which helps prevent escalation.

Recognizing and managing one's emotions to prevent escalation is vital for productive conversations. Start by identifying physical signs of stress, like a racing heart or clenched fists. Taking deep breaths or pausing before responding can help maintain composure. Sharing your feelings using "I" statements, such as "I feel stressed when deadlines approach," instead of blaming the other person, can also de-escalate tensions.

Developing emotional intelligence skills such as self-awareness and empathy allows for more effective conflict navigation. Self-awareness involves understanding your triggers and responses.
Reflecting on past conflicts can reveal patterns in how you react under stress. Combining this with empathy enables you to anticipate and address potential issues proactively.

Here is what you can do to enhance emotional intelligence:

- Set aside time for regular self-reflection to understand your emotional reactions.

- Practice mindfulness exercises to stay present and manage stress.

- Engage in activities that promote empathy, such as volunteering or learning about different cultures.

- Seek feedback from trusted friends or colleagues to gain insights into your behavioral patterns.

Key takeaways from incorporating empathy and emotional intelligence in conflict resolution are manifold. By applying empathy, you create an environment where all parties feel heard and respected, setting the stage for constructive dialogue.

Enhancing your emotional intelligence equips you with tools to remain calm and thoughtful during disputes. This dual approach fosters understanding, reduces the likelihood of conflicts escalating, and promotes collaborative solutions.

In conclusion, embracing empathy and emotional intelligence in conflict resolution transforms potentially volatile situations into opportunities for growth and connection. By actively practicing these principles, we pave the way for more meaningful and effective conversations that honor both individual experiences and collective well-being.

## Key takeaways

Throughout this chapter, we delved into various strategies for managing and resolving conflicts in a healthy manner. Understanding the common sources of conflict, such as miscommunication, differing expectations, and unresolved issues, sets the foundation for effective resolution. By recognizing these triggers and addressing them constructively, we can mitigate the escalation of disagreements.

We also explored different conflict resolution styles—compromising, collaborating, accommodating, competing, and avoiding—and their appropriate applications. Each style offers unique strengths depending on the context and relationship dynamics.

Flexibility in choosing and adapting these styles can lead to more favorable outcomes and prevent entrenchment in conflicts.

De-escalating tensions through practical techniques like breathing exercises, active listening, and taking breaks is essential during high-stress moments. These methods help keep emotions in check, facilitating clearer and calmer communication. Expressing thoughts and feelings using "I" statements fosters a non-confrontational dialogue, making it easier for both parties to engage openly.

Building compromise and consensus requires patience, empathy, and active listening. Valuing the relationship over individual positions fosters solutions that benefit everyone involved. This chapter emphasized that the goal of conflict resolution is not to win but to resolve, ensuring the longevity and health of relationships.

Enhancing communication skills further aids in effective conflict resolution. Active and reflective listening, using open-ended questions, and expressing emotions constructively are vital components. Assertive communication respects boundaries while ensuring clarity of needs and concerns.

As we've seen, managing non-verbal cues and practicing mindfulness help convey messages accurately, preventing misunderstandings. Open body language, controlled tone of voice, and attentive facial expressions contribute significantly to positive communication.

In summary, navigating conflicts effectively involves a combination of clear communication, flexibility, empathy, and mindfulness. Recognizing and addressing the root causes, adopting suitable resolution styles, and prioritizing the relationship underscore the importance of constructive conflict management. The skills and techniques discussed offer valuable tools for fostering healthier, more harmonious relationships.

As you apply these strategies, consider how they might transform not only your personal interactions but also the broader context of your relationships. In the quest for harmony, the ability to resolve conflicts constructively becomes an invaluable asset, paving the way for deeper connections and mutual understanding.

# References

Chastain, A. (2013, June). *Use your emotional intelligence to deal with others in conflict more effectively. MSU Extension.* https:// www.canr.msu.edu/news/

use_your_emotional_intelligence_to_deal_with_oth
ers_in_conflict_more_effect.

*Effective Communication is Key to Resolving Conflicts | Army and Navy Academy. Army and Navy Academy.* (n.d.). https://www.armyandnavyacademy.org/blog/effectivecommunication-is-key-to-resolving-conflicts/.

Hedstrom, R. (2018). *Coaching Through Conflict: Effective Communication Strategies | Association for Applied Sport Psychology. Appliedsportpsych.org.* https://appliedsportpsych.org/resources/resourcesfor-coaches/coaching-through-conflict-effectivecommunication-strategies/.

Krakoff, S. (2023, November). *The Top 5 Conflict Resolution Strategies for the Workplace. online.champlain.edu.* https://online.champlain.edu/blog/top-conflict-resolutionstrategies.

Laker, B., Pereira, V. (2022, May). *4 Triggers Cause the Majority of Team Conflicts. Harvard Business Review.* https://hbr.org/2022/05/conflict-is-notalways-bad-but-you-should-know-how-to-manage-it.


*principled negotiation. PON - Program on Negotiation at Harvard Law School.* (n.d.). https://www.pon.harvard.edu/tag/principled-negotiation/.

# Chapter Six

# The Science of Empathy

Empathy is more than a mere emotional response; it is the bridge that connects individuals on a deeper level. Throughout history, empathy has played a pivotal role in fostering understanding and cooperation among people. When we empathize, we effectively step into someone else's shoes, experiencing their emotions and viewpoints as if they were our own. This ability transforms how we interact with others, allowing us to build trust and form meaningful connections.

Despite its importance, many still struggle to practice empathy consistently. In everyday interactions, misunderstandings and conflicts can arise from a lack of empathetic engagement. For instance, a friend might feel unheard or dismissed because we fail to truly listen and validate their feelings. Similarly, workplace dynamics can suffer when team members overlook each other's perspectives, leading to disagreements and reduced collaboration. These scenarios underscore the critical need for developing empathy skills to improve our personal and professional relationships.

This chapter delves into the intricate science behind empathy and its profound impact on relationships. We will explore the neurological basis of empathy, including the role of neuroplasticity and mirror neurons in shaping our empathic responses. Additionally, we'll examine practical methods for enhancing empathy through active listening and mindfulness practices. By understanding these scientific insights and applying them to our daily lives, we can foster deeper, more meaningful connections with those around us, transforming the way we relate to others.

# Understanding the neuroscience of empathy and its impact on relationships

Exploring the role of empathy in creating deeper, more meaningful connections can fundamentally reshape how we relate to others. To start, let's delve into neuroplasticity and empathy. Practicing empathy isn't just a social or emotional act; it significantly impacts our brains. Engaging regularly in empathetic behaviors can rewire our neural pathways, promoting more compassionate responses. The brain's incredible ability to adapt through neuroplasticity means that empathy is a skill we can develop over time.

Understanding how the brain adapts to empathetic experiences helps us cultivate an empathic mindset in our relationships. Neuroscientific studies highlight that empathy is not purely innate but can be learned and honed with practice. This is empowering because it suggests anyone can improve their capacity for empathy, leading to richer emotional connections.

Neuroscientific findings further inform us that empathy can enhance our relationships on multiple levels. By developing neural pathways dedicated to empathy, we proactively build stronger emotional bonds with those around us. This process involves engaging deeply with others' experiences and emotions, which can fortify understanding and connection across all types of relationships.

Now, consider the role of the mirror neuron system in empathy and social bonding. Mirror neurons are specialized cells in the brain that activate both when we perform an action and when we observe others performing the same action. These neurons enable us to share and understand the emotions of others, fostering a natural empathic response. By recognizing how these neurons function, we can deepen our interactions and communication.

Leaning into this knowledge, cultivating mirror neuron activation can heighten emotional resonance and forge tighter interpersonal bonds. Here is what you can do:

- Practice mindfulness to become more attuned to your own and others' emotional states.

- Engage in active listening, ensuring you are fully present in conversations.

- Reflect others' emotions to show understanding and validation.

- Regularly put yourself in others' shoes to better grasp their perspectives.

By following these steps, you tap into the power of mirror neurons to strengthen your empathic abilities.

Exploring how empathy engages the brain's default mode network (DMN) also provides insights into our social cognition. The DMN activates when we ponder our thoughts, reflect on past interactions, or consider future social scenarios. Empathy stimulates regions within this network, making us more adept at understanding and feeling compassion for others.

This engagement bolsters our communication skills, as we're better equipped to appreciate others' viewpoints and respond thoughtfully. Leveraging these brain regions can thus promote harmonious relationships. In activating these empathic neural circuits, we foster a shared humanity and greater empathy in diverse contexts, from personal interactions to broader social dynamics.

As we piece all this together, it's clear that empathy isn't merely a soft skill—its roots are firmly planted in neuroscience. Understanding this empowers us to intentionally cultivate empathy, enhancing the quality of our connections and interactions. By recognizing the tangible effects of empathy on our brains and relationships, we can approach each interaction with a greater sense of purpose and compassion.

Empathy doesn't simply enrich relationships; it transforms them. Whether with partners, friends, family, or colleagues, practicing empathy lays the foundation for deeper, more meaningful connections, reinforcing our collective human experience.

# Highlighting the benefits of empathetic interactions for personal and professional relationships

Enhanced emotional connection

Empathy is a powerful tool that deepens emotional bonds between individuals, making our connections richer and more meaningful. By truly understanding and sharing someone else's feelings, we create a bond that goes beyond surface-level interactions. This emotional resonance helps nurture mutual understanding, paving the way for stronger, more intimate relationships.

Developing empathy can bridge emotional gaps and nurture greater intimacy in personal connections. Here is what you can do to achieve this:

- Take time to listen without interrupting, allowing others to express themselves fully.

- Try to put yourself in their shoes, imagining how you would feel in their situation.

- Validate their emotions by acknowledging their feelings and showing that you understand their perspective.

- Practice patience and avoid jumping to conclusions or offering unsolicited advice.

In professional settings, practicing empathy creates a more supportive and collaborative environment. When team members feel understood and valued, they are more likely to work together harmoniously, fostering a culture of teamwork and innovation.

Conflict resolution through empathy

Empathy can be a game-changer when it comes to resolving conflicts. By empowering us to see situations from others' perspectives, empathy encourages constructive dialogue and genuine understanding.

This approach helps reduce defensiveness, allowing for open communication and compromise.

Utilizing empathy in conflicts can reduce defensiveness and encourage open communication in relationships. Here's how you can employ empathy effectively:

- Approach conflicts with an open mind, ready to listen to the other person's point of view.

- Acknowledge their feelings and demonstrate that you understand their concerns.

- Seek common ground and be willing to find mutually acceptable solutions.

- Stay calm and composed, focusing on the issue rather than personal attacks.

Applying empathetic approaches leads to more effective problem-solving and long-lasting resolutions in relationships. It transforms potentially adversarial interactions into opportunities for growth and deeper connection.

Empathy as a relationship builder

Empathy is essential for building trust and rapport between individuals. When we practice empathy consistently, we establish a foundation of emotional safety and respect, crucial for healthy and thriving relationships. Authentic connections foster mutual respect, making our interactions more fulfilling and enriching.

Building a culture of empathy and understanding requires consistent effort and commitment.

Practicing empathy in all types of relationships can yield profound benefits. Here are some ways to cultivate empathy regularly:

- Make a habit of checking in emotionally with those around you.

- Show appreciation and gratitude for their efforts and contributions.

- Offer support and encouragement during challenging times.

- Lead by example, demonstrating empathy in your actions and interactions.

By doing so, we not only enhance our personal relationships but also contribute to a more empathetic and compassionate society.

Key takeaways

Understanding the transformative power of empathy is vital in nurturing emotionally rich and harmonious relationships. Through enhanced emotional connections, effective conflict resolution, and building strong relational foundations, empathy serves as a cornerstone for thriving interactions in every sphere of life. As we strive to incorporate empathy into our daily lives, we pave the way for deeper, more meaningful connections that stand the test of time.

# Providing insights into practical methods for enhancing empathy, particularly through empathic listening

Elements of empathic listening are at the heart of creating deeper, more meaningful connections. Attentive listening, empathy, and non-judgment are essential aspects that promote understanding between individuals. Reflective responses and validation during conversations are powerful tools in active listening, allowing us to show genuine empathy and deepen relationships. By engaging in empathic listening, we foster emotional intimacy and create a safe space for open communication.

Empathic listening is a practice that requires mindfulness and intention. To truly connect with another person, it's crucial to focus entirely on their words and feelings. Here's what you can do to engage in empathic listening:

- Demonstrate interest by maintaining eye contact and offering verbal affirmations.

- Paraphrase what the speaker says to ensure you understand their perspective.

- Reflect the speaker's feelings back to them, validating their emotions.

- Avoid distractions by putting away phones and minimizing background noise.

Practicing active listening can significantly improve our ability to communicate empathically. Some helpful tips include focusing on the speaker, setting an intention for the conversation, and being fully present. It's also beneficial to ask clarifying questions and avoid formulating your response while the other person is talking.

When paraphrasing, aim to mirror the speaker's words without judgment. This helps validate their feelings and promotes a deeper connection. Reflecting on their emotions shows that you genuinely care about how they feel, enhancing empathic resonance. By avoiding distractions and listening attentively, you can fully comprehend the speaker's perspective.

Active listening skills can be improved through consistent practice:

- Set clear intentions for every conversation to understand the speaker better.

- Practice mindful presence by eliminating distractions and focusing solely on the conversation.

- Ask thoughtful questions to delve deeper into the speaker's thoughts and emotions.

- Refrain from passing judgment, remaining open and neutral regardless of the topic.

The benefits of empathic listening are numerous and far-reaching. Employing empathic listening in relationships leads to enhanced mutual understanding and trust. This type of listening fosters emotional validation and creates a supportive environment where authentic communication thrives. Developing such skills results in more meaningful and fulfilling connections with others.

By honing empathic listening skills, individuals can pave the way for deeper emotional connections and empathetic relationships. As we practice these skills, we begin to build stronger bonds based on shared understanding and compassion. The positive outcomes of effective empathic listening practices extend beyond personal relationships, influencing professional interactions and community bonds as well.

Improving active listening skills involves persistence and dedication, but the rewards are immense. Start today by demonstrating genuine interest in your conversations. Focus on the speaker, reflect their feelings, and validate their experiences. With each interaction, you will find yourself becoming a better listener, more attuned to the emotions and needs of those around you.

In summary, empathic listening isn't just a skill—it's a transformative approach to building deeper, more meaningful connections. By practicing attentive listening, empathy, and non-judgment, we create spaces where emotional intimacy can flourish. Active listening techniques, such as paraphrasing and reflecting feelings, not only validate the speaker but also enhance our own capacity for understanding and empathy. Embracing empathic listening in our relationships leads to richer, more fulfilling connections, grounded in trust and mutual respect.

## Exploring the role of empathy in various types of relationships and its transformative potential

Empathy is a cornerstone of personal relationships, playing a vital role in strengthening bonds and fostering deeper connections. Empathy allows us to step into our partner's shoes, understanding their feelings, thoughts, and needs on a profound level. This shared emotional experience promotes closeness, helping couples navigate conflicts with greater ease and support one another through life's challenges. Research by Jenny Rickardsson suggests that high levels of empathy in relationships correlate with increased satisfaction and resilience (Rickardsson, J., n.d.).

Here is what you can do to foster empathy in your romantic relationship:

- Actively listen to your partner without interrupting.

- Reflect back what they share to show you understand their perspective.

- Validate their emotions even if you don't agree with their viewpoint.

- Show genuine interest in their day-to-day experiences.

Expressing empathy can deepen emotional intimacy. When we truly understand and feel our partner's emotions, it enhances our connection and trust. Regularly practicing empathy leads to a more harmonious and supportive partnership, reducing misunderstandings and building a solid foundation of mutual respect.

In social interactions, empathy enhances community bonds by promoting kindness and cooperation. Communities thrive when members practice empathy, creating an environment of inclusivity and compassion. By fostering understanding among individuals, empathy knits together a more cohesive and supportive social fabric.

To promote empathy in social settings:

- Take the time to genuinely listen to others' experiences.

- Avoid making judgments or assumptions about people's situations.

- Offer help and support where needed, showing care through actions.

- Create spaces where diverse voices are heard and valued.

Empathy at the workplace is crucial for fostering collaboration and teamwork. It promotes effective communication and smooth conflict resolution. Cultivating empathy leads to better team dynamics and a positive work environment where trust, respect, and camaraderie flourish. Empathetic leaders and colleagues build workplaces where everyone feels valued and understood, enhancing overall productivity and job satisfaction (Koukouli et al., 2020).

Here's how you can enhance empathy at work:

- Encourage open dialogue and active listening during meetings.

- Show appreciation for your colleagues' contributions and efforts.

- Address conflicts by acknowledging different viewpoints and finding common ground.

- Create a culture of feedback where everyone feels safe to express their thoughts.

Leveraging empathy at work means creating a supportive space where collaboration can thrive. Such environments see reduced stress and burnout, as employees feel more connected and understood. Empathy bridges gaps between team members, leading to innovative solutions and stronger professional ties.

Empathy's transformative power lies in its universality across different types of relationships. Whether it's personal, social, or professional, practicing empathy enriches connections by nurturing understanding and compassion. As we cultivate empathetic practices, we create spaces where every individual feels seen, heard, and valued, paving the way for more fulfilling relationships and communities.

**This detailed outline of Chapter 5: "The Science of Empathy" delves into the neurological underpinnings of empathy, its numerous benefits in interpersonal relationships, practical strategies for enhancing empathic connections, and the contextual application of empathy across personal, social, and professional relationship dynamics.**

Throughout this chapter, we have explored the significant role empathy plays in creating deeper and more meaningful connections. By understanding the neuroscience of empathy, we have seen how practicing empathetic behaviors can rewire our neural pathways, enhancing our ability to form compassionate responses. Neuroplasticity shows us that empathy is a skill we can develop over time, making it accessible to everyone willing to practice.

We delved into how empathy strengthens relationships on multiple levels. By engaging deeply with others' experiences and emotions, we fortify understanding and connections across all types of relationships. The activation of mirror neurons helps us share and understand the emotions of others, fostering natural empathic responses. This knowledge allows us to deepen interactions and communication, promoting tighter interpersonal bonds.

Furthermore, we discussed how empathy engages the brain's default mode network (DMN), which is crucial for social cognition. Stimulating regions within this network makes us more adept at feeling compassion for others, thereby enhancing our communication skills and appreciating different viewpoints. These neural engagements emphasize that empathy is not just an emotional act but a scientifically-backed method to cultivate harmonious relationships.

Empathy's power extends to both personal and professional settings. In personal relationships, it bridges emotional gaps and nurtures intimacy. In professional environments, empathy fosters a supportive culture that encourages teamwork and collaboration. By practicing empathy, we create spaces where individuals feel understood and valued, paving the way for innovative solutions and stronger connections.

As we recognize the tangible effects of empathy on our brains and relationships, it becomes clear that empathy transforms interactions, laying a foundation for enriched human experiences. Leveraging these insights empowers us to approach each interaction with greater purpose and compassion.

In essence, empathy doesn't merely enhance relationships—it transforms them. Whether with partners, friends, family, or colleagues, integrating empathy into our daily lives reinforces our collective human experience. As we continue to cultivate empathy, we build a more connected and compassionate world, one interaction at a time.

# References

*7 Ways To Improve Your Active Listening Skills. Cleveland Clinic.* (2023, May). https://health.clevelandclinic.org/active-listening.

Coursera Staff. (2022, May). *7 Active Listening Techniques to Communicate Better. Coursera.* https://www.coursera.org/articles/active-listening.

Klimecki, O., Lamm, C., Leiberg, S., Singer, T. (2012, June). *Functional Neural Plasticity and Associated*

Changes in Positive Affect After Compassion Training. *Cerebral Cortex.* https://greatergood.berkeley.edu/images/uploads/KlimeckiPositiveAffectCompassionTraining.pdf.

Klimecki, O., Leiberg, S., Ricard, M., Singer, T. (2013, May). *Differential pattern of functional brain plasticity after compassion and empathy training. Social Cognitive and Affective Neuroscience.* https://academic.oup.com/scan/article/9/6/873/1669505.

Koukouli, S., Moudatsou, M., Philalithis, A., Stavropoulou, A. (2020, January). *The Role of Empathy in Health and Social Care Professionals. Healthcare.* https://www.ncbi.nlm.nih.gov/pmc/articles/PMC7151200/.

Rickardsson, J. (n.d.). *Stiftelsen 29k Foundation. 29k.org.* https://29k.org/article/5-reasons-whyempathy-is-important-in-relationships.

Ringwald, W., Wright, A. (2020, December). *The Affiliative Role of Empathy in Everyday*

*Interpersonal Interactions. European Journal of Personality.* https://doi.org/10.1002%2Fper.2286.

# Chapter Seven

# The Foundations of Strong Relationships

When we consider the many facets of human relationships, trust and respect often emerge as indispensable elements. Imagine a friendship where promises are routinely broken or a partnership lacking in mutual regard; such connections tend to falter and dissolve over time. Trust and respect are not mere niceties but essential building blocks that make relationships strong and enduring. Their presence fosters an environment where individuals feel safe, valued, and understood, laying the groundwork for deep and meaningful connections.

The absence of trust can lead to significant relational issues. Without it, interactions are fraught with suspicion, insecurity, and constant worry. For example, if a friend frequently cancels plans at the last minute, it may breed feelings of unreliability and doubt. Over time, these small fractures can grow into larger rifts. Similarly, respect plays a crucial role in maintaining a healthy relationship. Disrespect manifests in various forms, such as dismissing someone's feelings or belittling their opinions, leading to emotional disconnection and resentment. When individuals do not feel respected, they are less likely to open up, resulting in a lack of genuine communication and understanding.

This chapter delves into how trust and respect form the bedrock of strong relationships. We will explore real-life examples and scientific explanations to illustrate the significance of these elements. Practical strategies for building and sustaining trust, fostering mutual respect, and navigating conflicts will be discussed. By the end of this chapter, you will gain valuable insights into creating and maintaining healthy, fulfilling relationships, whether with partners, friends, or family members. Through consistent effort and a genuine commitment to valuing each other, strong relationships can indeed withstand and flourish amid life's many challenges.

## The Concept and Importance of Trust

Trust is an essential component in any significant relationship, forming the foundation that underpins every meaningful connection. At its core, trust represents the belief in the reliability, truth, ability, or strength of someone or something. This belief allows individuals to be open and vulnerable in their interactions, fostering a sense of security and mutual respect.

When we trust someone, it permits us to feel secure in our relationships, whether with friends, family members, or partners. Trust means knowing that our confidences will remain safe, promises will be kept, and actions will align with words. It grants us the freedom to share our true selves without fear of judgment or betrayal.

Conversely, a lack of trust can lead to significant challenges. Without trust, communication often breaks down, leaving gaps filled with suspicion and doubt. Misunderstandings become more frequent, and emotional disconnection can occur. The once secure feeling in a relationship is replaced by uncertainty, making it difficult to maintain a healthy dynamic.

Given its critical role, nurturing trust should be a priority in all relationships. Here are practical methods to build and sustain trust:

- Communication Transparency: Being open and honest in your conversations is vital. Share your thoughts and feelings genuinely, even when it's challenging. This transparency fosters understanding and deepens trust.

- Consistency: Consistent actions over time build trust. When people see that you reliably follow through on your commitments, they learn to depend on you.

- Honesty: Avoid deceit or half-truths. While complete honesty requires courage, it is essential for sustaining trust. Lies, even small ones, can undermine the foundation of trust you've worked hard to build.

- Setting and Respecting Boundaries: Clear boundaries create a sense of safety and predictability in relationships. Respect each other's limits, and ensure that both parties understand and honor these boundaries.

- Demonstrating Reliability: Show that you can be counted on in various circumstances. Keep your word, meet deadlines, and be present when needed. Reliability isn't about being perfect but rather showing consistent effort and dependability.

By applying these strategies, you lay the groundwork for lasting trust, which benefits all aspects of your relationship, from day-to-day interactions to handling conflicts and misunderstandings. Trust takes time to develop, but with dedicated effort and genuine intentions, it can become the bedrock of your most cherished connections.

As we reflect on trust and its myriad impacts, it becomes evident that cultivating this quality goes beyond mere actions. It's about creating an environment where everyone feels valued, heard, and safe to express themselves. With trust deeply embedded, relationships can weather adversities, adapt to changes, and flourish even amid challenges.

In summary, trust serves as the foundational pillar for strong relationships, offering a secure space for openness and vulnerability. By embracing transparency, consistency, honesty, respect for boundaries, and reliability, we foster trust that not only sustains but also enriches our connections. Whether with partners, friends, or family, investing in trust helps build lasting, meaningful relationships marked by mutual respect and deep understanding.

# Mutual Respect and Relationship Health

Mutual respect is the cornerstone of any strong relationship. It begins with recognizing each individual's worth and dignity, understanding that every person brings unique value to the table. When we treat others with consideration, empathy, and fairness, we lay the foundation for healthy interactions. Respect involves acknowledging boundaries and differences while valuing each other's perspectives, which enhances harmony and reduces conflicts.

Disrespect, on the other hand, can significantly erode trust and create emotional distance. When someone feels disrespected, it can lead to feelings of insecurity and resentment, making it difficult to maintain a close connection. Therefore, cultivating mutual respect is essential for sustaining trust and intimacy in relationships.

Rebuilding trust after breaches can be challenging but not impossible. Here are some strategies for repairing trust when it has been compromised:

- Acknowledge the breach. Recognizing the occurrence and taking responsibility for one's actions is the first crucial step.

- Open communication. Engage in honest conversations about what happened and how it affected both parties.

- Offer genuine apologies. Express sincere regret and show an understanding of the impact caused by the breach.

- Consistent efforts. Demonstrate commitment through ongoing efforts to rebuild trust and make positive changes.

- Time and patience. Understand that rebuilding trust is a gradual process that requires patience and dedication from both sides.

To sum up, mutual respect forms the bedrock of strong relationships by promoting understanding, empathy, and fairness. When respect is present, trust flourishes, and connections deepen. In cases where trust has been broken, deliberate actions and consistent effort can pave the way for healing and strengthening bonds. By appreciating each other's worth and maintaining open, respectful dialogue, relationships can navigate challenges and grow stronger over time.

(Bay, C., n.d.)

# Trust, Respect, and Conflict Resolution

Navigating conflicts with trust involves recognizing how trust serves as a foundation for resolving disagreements constructively. When trust is present, individuals can engage in difficult conversations with honesty and vulnerability. This openness helps both parties to explore the core issues without fear of deception or ulterior motives. Trust allows individuals to acknowledge mistakes, express concerns, and make amends, fostering an environment conducive to genuine dialogue.

Mutual respect plays a crucial role in creating a supportive atmosphere where disagreements can be addressed respectfully. With respect, even contentious topics can be tackled with sensitivity and understanding. Respecting each other's perspectives enables partners to discuss differing viewpoints without feeling dismissed or belittled. This mutual consideration paves the way for healthy discourse, making it possible to find common ground and solutions that are acceptable to all involved.

Building trust ensures that conflicts are approached without fear of judgment or rejection. When partners have faith in each other's intentions, they are more likely to interpret actions and words in a positive light. This reduces misunderstandings and promotes a cooperative spirit in resolving issues. Trust creates a psychological safety net, encouraging open communication and reducing defensiveness.

Conflict resolution through mutual respect requires specific strategies to ensure both personal dignity and relational harmony. Here is what you can do to uphold respect while resolving conflicts:

- Practice active listening, which involves genuinely hearing and understanding the other person's point of view without interrupting.

- Use empathy to validate the other person's feelings and experiences, demonstrating that their emotions are acknowledged and valued.

- Find common ground by identifying shared goals and values, which can serve as a foundation for compromise and collaboration.

- Focus on the issue at hand rather than resorting to personal attacks or bringing up past grievances.

- Approach the conversation with a problem-solving mindset, seeking solutions that benefit both parties rather than insisting on being right.

A key tactic in respecting oneself and others during conflict resolution is active listening. By attentively listening, empathizing, and validating one another's experiences, conflicts can be de-escalated and mutual understanding fostered. For instance, giving each other the time and space to explain their side without interruptions shows respect and patience, laying the groundwork for productive discussions.

Finding common ground is another vital component. This involves focusing on shared goals and values, which can bridge differences and promote mutual respect. By emphasizing what both parties agree on, it becomes easier to move forward together, despite individual disagreements. This approach also highlights the importance of compromise and collaboration, showing that progress is made through partnership rather than opposition.

Ultimately, you will learn how integral trust and mutual respect are to effective conflict resolution. These elements promote understanding and harmony in relationships, encouraging partners to address conflicts constructively and empathetically. Maintaining these principles allows for healthier interactions and deeper emotional connections, ensuring that relationships can withstand and grow from challenges.

In summary, trust and respect are essential in navigating conflicts and maintaining strong relationships. They enable honest communication, foster a respectful environment, and provide a foundation for resolving disputes constructively. By practicing active listening, empathy, and finding common ground, individuals can address conflicts effectively, promoting lasting understanding and harmony.

## Long-Term Impact of Trust and Mutual Respect

Trust and respect are the cornerstones of strong, enduring relationships. When both elements are present, they form a powerful foundation that supports lasting bonds between partners, friends, and family members. Let's dive into how trust and mutual respect contribute to relationship sustainability over the long term.

Sustaining trust and respect in relationships requires proactive efforts. Here is what you can do to maintain these crucial elements over time:

- Consistently communicate with your partner or friend about your thoughts, feelings, and experiences. This keeps the lines of communication open and helps prevent misunderstandings.

- Validate each other's feelings and experiences. Acknowledging and empathizing with what the other person is going through reinforces that their emotions are valued and respected.

- Show appreciation regularly. Simple expressions of gratitude can go a long way in reinforcing positive feelings and mutual respect.

Consistent communication, validation, and appreciation play a significant role in reinforcing trust and respect. One of the most effective ways to build and maintain these elements in a relationship is through continual efforts to understand and support each other. By actively listening and showing empathy, you can create a deep sense of connection and emotional intimacy.

It's also essential to address issues promptly, honestly, and empathetically. When problems arise, avoiding them or sweeping them under the rug can lead to resentment and misunderstandings. Instead, bring up concerns as soon as they occur, and do so with a caring and respectful attitude. Discussing issues openly not only prevents small problems from escalating but also strengthens the trust and respect in your relationship by demonstrating a commitment to resolving conflicts constructively.

By understanding and implementing these strategies, you can see the enduring significance of trust and mutual respect in sustaining healthy, fulfilling relationships. It's this continuous effort and mutual understanding that form the bedrock of any successful relationship, ensuring it remains robust and resilient through life's many challenges.

# Conclusion of the Chapter

This chapter has delved into the critical roles of trust and respect in forming and sustaining strong relationships. We've explored the fundamental nature of trust—its importance in providing a sense of security and mutual respect, and the detrimental effects of its absence. Trust enables open communication and vulnerability, allowing individuals to share their true selves without fear of judgment or betrayal. Conversely, a lack of trust can lead to communication breakdowns and emotional disconnection.

Earlier, we discussed how nurturing trust is essential for building healthy relationships. Consistency, honesty, transparent communication, and respecting boundaries were highlighted as key methods for fostering trust. By applying these strategies, one can create a solid foundation for lasting connections marked by reliability and dependability.

Mutual respect was also underscored as the cornerstone of relationship health. Respecting each other's worth and dignity promotes harmony and reduces conflicts. When trust is breached, rebuilding it requires acknowledgment, open communication, genuine apologies, consistent efforts, and patience. Through these deliberate actions, it is possible to heal and strengthen bonds.

The chapter further examined how trust and mutual respect are vital for effective conflict resolution. Trust allows for honest and vulnerable conversations, reducing misunderstandings and promoting a cooperative spirit. Mutual respect ensures that even contentious issues are addressed with sensitivity and understanding, facilitating the discovery of common ground and collaborative solutions.

Sustaining trust and mutual respect over the long term involves consistent communication, validation of feelings, and regular expressions of appreciation. Addressing issues promptly and empathetically prevents small problems from escalating and demonstrates a commitment to resolving conflicts constructively.

In summary, trust and mutual respect are indispensable for building and maintaining strong relationships. They foster open communication, create a supportive environment for conflict resolution, and ensure the longevity and health of connections. By embracing these principles, relationships can weather adversities, adapt to changes, and flourish over time. The continuous effort to understand and support each other remains the bedrock of successful, enduring relationships.

# References

Ahmad, S., Ghauri, T., Jahangir, M., Kiran, A., Riaz, S., Toseef, M., Ullah, I., Wei, Z., Zhuo, S. (2022, July). *Inspirational Leadership and Innovative Communication in Sustainable Organizations: A*

*Mediating Role of Mutual Trust. Frontiers in Psychology.* None.

Bartley, L., Boaz, A., Farley, A., Jensen, T., Metz, A., Villodas, M. (2022, September). *Building trusting relationships to support implementation: A proposed theoretical model. Frontiers in Health Services.* https://www.ncbi.nlm.nih.gov/pmc/articles/PMC10012819/.

Bay, C. (n.d.). *Cultivating Mutual Respect. csumb.edu.* https://csumb.edu/hr/employeedevelopment/pearls-of-wisdom/cultivating-mutualrespect/.

Ellis, V., Ronquillo, Y., Toney-Butler, T. (2023, July). *Conflict Management. National Library of Medicine.* https://www.ncbi.nlm.nih.gov/books/NBK470432/.

Krakoff, S. (2023, November). *The Top 5 Conflict Resolution Strategies for the Workplace. online.champlain.edu.* https://

<u>online.champlain.edu/blog/top-conflict-resolutionstrategies.</u>

Chapter Eight

# The Influence of Culture and Society

Relationships are as diverse as the cultures and societies that shape them. From family structures to friendship norms, the way we connect with others is deeply influenced by our cultural backgrounds and societal expectations. This chapter delves into the intriguing ways these factors impact our interactions and relationships, providing a window into the complex world of social dynamics.

One key challenge in understanding relationships across different cultures is recognizing how deeply ingrained cultural norms and traditions can be. For example, in some cultures, collectivism emphasizes community and familial decision-making, while individual autonomy is celebrated in others. These differing values can create both harmony and conflict in relationships, depending on how they are navigated. Furthermore, cultural traditions dictate practices ranging from gender roles to marriage rituals, which can uphold continuity but also impose restrictions. Cross-cultural relationships add another layer of complexity, requiring partners to bridge gaps and blend diverse perspectives. Stereotypes and biases further complicate matters by creating misconceptions that hinder genuine connections. By examining these examples, the chapter highlights the myriad ways culture and society shape how we relate to one another.

In the following sections, this chapter will explore several critical areas. It will delve into how cultural diversity influences relationship norms, showcasing specific cultural practices and their impacts. The influence of tradition on relationships will be examined, with practical tips for evaluating and adapting these customs. The chapter will also discuss the dynamics of cross-cultural relationships, offering strategies for fostering understanding and respect. Lastly, it will address the role of stereotypes and biases, suggesting ways to overcome these barriers for more inclusive and respectful connections. Through this exploration, you will gain insights and tools to navigate relationships more effectively in today's culturally diverse world.

# Exploring the variations in relationship dynamics across different cultures and societies.

Understanding how cultural and societal norms shape our relationships is essential in today's interconnected world. Relationships are influenced by various factors, including cultural diversity, traditions, cross-cultural interactions, and stereotypes. To navigate these elements effectively, we need to appreciate diverse perspectives, challenge constraints, and foster genuine connections.

Cultural Diversity in Relationship Norms: Different cultures have unique ways of perceiving and navigating relationship structures. For instance, some cultures emphasize collectivism, where family and community play a significant role in decision-making, while others focus on individual autonomy. Understanding these cultural frameworks helps us appreciate the diversity in relationship dynamics, promoting empathy and respect.

Influence of Tradition on Relationships: Cultural traditions significantly shape relationship rituals and expectations within communities. Traditions can dictate everything from gender roles to marriage practices. While these customs provide a sense of continuity and identity, they can sometimes be restrictive. Overcoming traditional constraints can lead to personal growth and deeper connections.

Here is what you can do to achieve this:

- Evaluate the traditions influencing your relationships.

- Discuss openly with your partner or family about which traditions feel supportive versus those that feel limiting.

- Seek mutual agreements on how to honor or adapt these traditions.

- Allow space for new, shared traditions that reflect both partners' values and beliefs.

Cross-Cultural Relationships: Relationships between individuals from different cultural backgrounds are complex but rewarding. Navigating cultural differences fosters adaptability and open-mindedness. To thrive in such relationships, consider these steps:

- Engage in open and honest communication about cultural expectations and practices.

- Show willingness to understand and respect each other's backgrounds.

- Be patient and flexible, understanding that cultural adaptation takes time.

Challenging Stereotypes in Relationships: Stereotypes can hinder authentic connections by creating misconceptions and biases. Addressing these biases is crucial for fostering genuine understanding.

Breaking stereotypes fosters meaningful relationships. Here is what you can do to achieve this:

- Reflect on your own biases and educate yourself about their origins.

- Seek firsthand experiences and conversations with people from diverse backgrounds.

- Practice active listening and empathy in all interactions.

- Challenge biased remarks and behaviors in social settings respectfully.

Overcoming biases enhances communication and fosters inclusive relationships. When we actively work towards bias-free interactions, we create a more inclusive environment that strengthens our bonds with others.

In summary, appreciating cultural diversity and traditions in relationships promotes empathy and understanding. Navigating cross-cultural complexities fosters adaptability and broadens our outlook. By challenging stereotypes and overcoming biases, we build inclusive, respectful, and authentic connections. Understanding how cultural and societal norms shape our relationships leads to greater empathy, adaptability, and inclusive interactions, ultimately fostering stronger and more fulfilling relationships.

# Exploring the impact of societal norms on individual relationships and behaviors.

Understanding how cultural and societal norms shape our relationships can be enlightening. Social expectations play a crucial role in shaping relationship roles and expectations. From early on, we are conditioned to follow certain behaviors appropriate for specific situations. Each social situation comes with a set of expected behaviors, which vary between different groups or communities (Mcleod, S., 2023). Understanding these pressures can help individuals navigate relationships more authentically.

To handle societal pressures and foster authentic connections:

- Reflect on how societal expectations influence your behavior.

- Identify which expectations align with your values and discard those that don't.

- Communicate openly with your partner about these realizations, creating a shared understanding.

Questioning societal norms allows us to challenge the status quo and seek more fulfilling connections. By stepping outside traditional molds, we open the door to empowerment and deeper relationships.

Community values also significantly influence interpersonal interactions. Being part of a community often means aligning personal values with communal expectations, which can enhance relationship satisfaction. Balancing individual autonomy with community values requires a nuanced approach.

Here's how to balance individual autonomy with community values:

- Understand the core values of your community.

- Recognize your own values and where they align or diverge from those of your community.

- Have open discussions with your partner about how to respect both individual and communal values.

This alignment fosters harmony and builds a supportive environment where relationships can thrive.

In discussing norms versus individuality, it's essential to strike a balance between conforming to societal expectations and expressing one's true self. Embracing personal values while respecting social norms promotes authenticity within relationships. Negotiating societal pressures helps in forming a strong self-identity and healthier relationships.

Consider these steps to negotiate societal pressures:

- Evaluate which norms support your personal growth and which ones inhibit it.

- Practice assertiveness in expressing your individuality.

- Encourage mutual respect for each other's individuality in your relationship.

Breaking free from societal molds can lead to significant personal growth. Challenging these constraints liberates individuals, fostering empowerment and nurturing deeper connections. When individuals embrace their unique identities within relationships, it promotes mutual respect and better understanding.

To experience empowerment and deeper connections:

- Encourage yourself and your partner to discuss and pursue personal aspirations.

- Support each other in deviating from unnecessary societal expectations.

- Celebrate individuality as a strength within your relationship.

By navigating these societal influences thoughtfully, we can create a strong foundation for authentic and fulfilling connections. Recognizing the interplay between societal norms and personal relationships empowers us to foster meaningful connections while navigating societal pressures. This balanced approach ultimately leads to more enriching and genuine relationships.

# Investigating the complexities of relationships in diverse cultural settings.

Cultural Adaptability in Relationships: Understanding the importance of adaptability in multicultural relationships

Flexibility and willingness to understand different cultures enhance relationship resilience. Every culture brings its own set of values, traditions, and ways of thinking. In a multicultural relationship, being adaptable isn't just beneficial; it's essential for the relationship's success. Adapting can mean learning about your partner's cultural background, celebrating their traditions, or even trying out new foods. Here is what you can do to achieve cultural adaptability:

- Be curious and open-minded. Engage with your partner's culture with genuine interest.

- Listen actively and ask questions to understand their perspective better.

- Show respect for their traditions and practices, even if they differ from your own.

- Be willing to compromise and blend cultures, creating new traditions together.

Navigating cultural differences requires open communication and mutual respect. To navigate these differences smoothly, communication plays a pivotal role. Clear, honest conversations help prevent misunderstandings and build trust. It's crucial to discuss expectations and boundaries openly. For instance, differing views on family involvement can lead to conflicts if not addressed early on.

Empathy bridges cultural divides and fosters deeper connections. When partners empathize with each other's experiences, they can better navigate cultural nuances. Empathy involves recognizing and validating your partner's feelings. This connection strengthens when both partners feel understood and appreciated. Cultivating empathy includes making an effort to see things from your partner's cultural viewpoint.

Effective communication strategies help navigate misinterpretations in intercultural relationships. Misunderstandings are common in any relationship but can be magnified in cross-cultural contexts. Developing effective communication strategies is key. Some useful strategies include:

- Use clear and concise language, avoiding slang or idiomatic expressions that might not translate well.

- Confirm understanding by paraphrasing what your partner has said and asking for clarification if needed.

- Be patient and give each other time to express thoughts fully.

- Approach miscommunications as opportunities to learn rather than sources of conflict.

Benefits of Cultural Exchange in Relationships: Exploring the enriching experiences gained from diverse cultural interactions

Learning from different cultures broadens perspectives and enriches relationship dynamics. Exposure to various cultures doesn't just broaden individual minds; it also enriches the relationship by creating unique dynamics. These experiences can be as simple as learning a new dance or as complex as understanding a different approach to life.

Cultural exchange fosters growth, tolerance, and mutual appreciation in relationships. Engaging in cultural exchange creates fertile ground for personal growth and strengthens the bond between partners. It helps develop tolerance and appreciation for diversity. Here's how you can foster this environment:

- Share stories and traditions from your cultural backgrounds.

- Attend cultural events or festivals together.

- Read books or watch movies from each other's cultures.

- Encourage discussions about cultural experiences and their impacts on each other's lives.

Challenges and Rewards in Intercultural Relationships: Addressing the obstacles faced and rewards reaped in intercultural relationships

Overcoming challenges in intercultural relationships leads to personal and relational growth. Intercultural relationships come with their fair share of challenges, such as differing social norms and familial expectations. Tackling these challenges head-on fosters growth. Each challenge faced and overcome strengthens the relationship, teaching resilience and deepening the emotional bond.

Shared experiences and cultural learning create a foundation for lasting and meaningful connections. The shared journey of navigating cultural differences builds a strong foundation for lasting and meaningful connections. These shared experiences deepen mutual understanding and add layers of meaning to the relationship.

By developing cultural competence, you can learn strategies for navigating the complexities of intercultural relationships, fostering empathy, understanding, and growth in diverse cultural settings. The key to thriving in a multicultural relationship lies in the willingness to adapt, communicate openly, and appreciate the richness that different cultures bring.

# Addressing biases, stereotypes, and prejudices that can hinder relationship development.

Challenging Stereotypes in Relationships

Stereotypes can silently sabotage our relationships. They create invisible barriers that distort interactions, preventing genuine connections. Research has shown that even subtle adjustments based on stereotypes can influence how we communicate and perceive each other (Bašnáková et al., 2023). For instance, assuming someone is less competent because of their age or background may unconsciously alter our behavior towards them, leading to misunderstandings and weakened bonds.

Recognizing and addressing stereotypes fosters authentic and inclusive connections. Here's what you can do:

- Reflect on your assumptions about others and question their validity.

- Engage in active listening to understand different perspectives.

- Cultivate empathy by placing yourself in others' shoes.

- Educate yourself on the diverse experiences and backgrounds of those around you.

Overcoming biases leads to more meaningful and respectful relationships. A crucial step is acknowledging that everyone, including ourselves, carries biases. By facing these biases head-on, we can work towards reducing their impact. This self-awareness transforms relationships into spaces of respect and mutual growth.

Roots of Bias in Relationships

Biases often stem from deep-rooted societal norms and personal experiences. Understanding these roots is essential for fostering self-reflection and growth in relationships. When we become aware of why we hold certain beliefs, we can better challenge them and open ourselves up to new ways of thinking.

Addressing biases can lead to enhanced empathy, communication, and relationship satisfaction. Recognizing our biases allows us to empathize with others' experiences and improve how we communicate. This, in turn, results in stronger, more satisfying relationships as barriers dissolve and genuine understanding emerges.

Promoting Inclusivity and Respect

Creating inclusive environments in relationships is vital. Embracing diversity and respecting individual differences strengthen relationship bonds. Imagine a world where every interaction is met with curiosity rather than judgment. Such an environment not only makes people feel valued but also enriches the relationship by bringing in varied perspectives and ideas.

Cultivating an inclusive mindset fosters mutual understanding and acceptance in relationships. To achieve this:

- Celebrate differences instead of perceiving them as threats.

- Encourage open dialogue about diverse experiences and viewpoints.

- Practice patience and openness when encountering unfamiliar customs or beliefs.

Tools for Overcoming Bias

Developing awareness of one's biases is the first step towards fostering bias-free connections. Here are practical strategies:

- Keep a journal of your interactions and note any biased thoughts or behaviors.

- Seek feedback from trusted friends or colleagues about your interactions.

- Participate in workshops or training sessions focused on diversity and inclusion.

Implementing inclusive practices leads to more harmonious and genuine relationships. As we actively work towards inclusivity, we begin to see relationships blossom in unexpected and beautiful ways. These efforts are not just about being politically correct; they are about building a world where everyone feels seen, heard, and valued.

In conclusion, recognizing and overcoming biases, stereotypes, and prejudices in relationships is crucial for fostering inclusivity, respect, and authentic connections. By challenging our assumptions, promoting diversity, and continually striving for self-awareness, we can create stronger, more meaningful relationships that reflect the best of humanity.

# Summarize the cultural and societal influences on relationships.

Throughout this chapter, we have explored the intricate ways cultural and societal norms shape our relationships. From understanding diverse relationship dynamics across different cultures to challenging the stereotypes that hinder genuine connections, it's clear that these influences are pervasive and profound.

Initially, we discussed how cultural diversity affects relationship norms. By appreciating various cultural frameworks, we can foster empathy and respect in our interactions. The influence of traditions was another key point. While traditions provide identity and continuity, evaluating and discussing them openly with loved ones can lead to personal growth and stronger bonds.

Cross-cultural relationships were highlighted as complex yet rewarding, emphasizing the need for open communication and mutual respect when navigating diverse backgrounds. Stereotypes also play a significant role in shaping relationships. Reflecting on and addressing our biases can lead to more meaningful and inclusive connections.

Understanding societal pressures and questioning societal norms allow individuals to navigate relationships authentically. Balancing individual autonomy with community values enhances relationship satisfaction and fosters harmony. Negotiating societal expectations helps form a strong self-identity and healthier relationships by promoting authenticity.

In exploring multicultural relationships, adaptability and effective communication emerged as critical factors. This adaptability encourages us to celebrate and integrate aspects of each other's cultures, enriching our relationships. Addressing challenges and embracing the rewards of intercultural relationships leads to personal and relational growth, creating lasting and meaningful connections.

Challenging stereotypes and recognizing the roots of biases in relationships promote inclusivity and respect. Developing awareness of one's biases and implementing inclusive practices lead to harmonious and genuine relationships. Celebrating differences and encouraging open dialogue about diverse experiences strengthen relationship bonds.

Ultimately, appreciating cultural diversity, navigating societal expectations thoughtfully, and fostering inclusive environments pave the way for authentic and fulfilling relationships. By understanding how cultural and societal norms shape our interactions, we can create connections built on empathy, adaptability, and mutual respect. These efforts ultimately enrich our lives and contribute to stronger, more resilient relationships.

# References


Axner, M. (2018). *Chapter 27. Cultural Competence in a Multicultural World | Section 2. Building Relationships with People from Different Cultures | Main Section | Community Tool Box. Ku.edu.* https://ctb.ku.edu/en/table-of-contents/culture/cultural-competence/building-relationships/main.

Bhatia, A., Bonell, C., Kohli, A., Kyegombe, N., Meiksin, R., Melendez-Torres, G. (2023, February). *Social Norms About Dating and Relationship Violence and Gender Among Adolescents:*

*Systematic Review of Measures Used in Dating and Relationship Violence Research. Trauma, Violence, & Abuse.* None.

Booth, J., Marsiglia, F. (2014, May). *Cultural Adaptation of Interventions in Real Practice Settings. Research on Social Work Practice.* https://www.ncbi.nlm.nih.gov/pmc/articles/PMC4512185/.

Drach-Zahavy, A., Endevelt, R., Sheffer Hilel, G. (2023, March). *The paradoxical effects of professional stereotypes on the quality of care by interprofessional teams: The contingent effects of team faultlines, team stereotypes, and championship behaviors. Frontiers in Psychology.* None.

Koch, S. B. J., Tyborowska, A., Niermann, H. C. M., Cillessen, A. H. N., Roelofs, K., Bašnáková, J., Toni, I., & Stolk, A. (2023). *Integrating stereotypes and factual evidence in interpersonal communication . bioRxiv .* https://doi.org/10.1101/2023.05.23.540979

Mcleod, S. (2023, April). *Social Roles and Social Norms | Simply Psychology. Simplypsychology.org.* https://www.simplypsychology.org/social-roles.html

.

# Chapter Nine

# Practical Exercises for Connection

Building strong relationships requires more than just good intentions; it demands tangible actions and practices that foster deeper connections. Imagine being able to navigate your interactions with loved ones in a way that not only strengthens your bonds but also enriches your understanding of each other. This chapter offers practical exercises designed to enhance your relationship skills through hands-on activities, allowing you to connect more genuinely and effectively with those around you.

One common issue in relationships is the lack of self-awareness and understanding of personal emotions, which can create misunderstandings and conflicts. For instance, consider moments when conversations with a partner or friend turned sour because you weren't fully aware of your own emotional triggers or communication patterns. By engaging in activities such as journaling for self-discovery, reflecting on past interactions, and practicing gratitude, individuals can better understand their feelings and reactions. These exercises encourage introspection and personal growth, providing a solid foundation for healthier interactions and deeper emotional connections.

In this chapter, we will explore various hands-on activities aimed at improving relationship skills. You'll learn how regular journaling can help uncover emotional patterns, how mindfulness practices like meditation and breathing exercises can promote present-moment awareness, and how role-playing scenarios can enhance communication abilities. Additionally, the chapter will delve into expressive arts and group reflections as tools for team cohesion and mutual support. By incorporating these practical exercises into your daily routine, you will be equipped with the skills needed to cultivate meaningful relationships built on empathy, understanding, and effective communication.

# Providing tools for self-reflection and deepening self-awareness to improve relationships.

Offering hands-on activities to enhance relationship skills can lead to deeper, more meaningful connections with those around us. One effective approach is journaling for self-discovery and connection. By engaging in regular journaling prompts, you can explore personal thoughts and emotions in a structured way.

To get started:

- Set aside a dedicated time each day for journaling. It doesn't have to be long; even 5-10 minutes can make a difference.

- Use open-ended prompts such as "I am aware that...", "What motivates me is...", or "Today, I aspire to...". Allow your thoughts to flow without judgment (Schoonover, J., n.d.).

Reflecting on past interactions is another powerful practice. This helps identify patterns and triggers in relationships. Look back at conversations or events where you felt strong emotions. Ask yourself what triggered those feelings and how you responded. Writing about these experiences allows you to gain clarity and make conscious changes moving forward.

Practicing gratitude and self-compassion fosters a positive mindset. Here are some steps to integrate these practices into your daily routine:

- Each morning or evening, jot down three things you're grateful for. These can be simple, like enjoying a cup of coffee or receiving a kind message from a friend.

- When facing challenges, write about them with a tone of self-compassion. Acknowledge your feelings and remind yourself that it's okay to have tough days.

Journaling exercises for expressing emotions effectively and understanding personal values can be transformative. To practice this:

- Choose topics that resonate deeply with you, such as "What hurts me is..." or "Love is...".

- Write freely for several minutes, allowing all your emotions to come to the surface. Don't worry about grammar or structure—just let the words flow.

The benefits of journaling are well-documented. Studies show that writing about emotional experiences can improve mood and physiological well-being (admin, 2014). As you continue this practice, you'll likely notice an enhanced ability to communicate authentically and empathize with others.

Engaging in these journaling activities can contribute significantly to self-discovery and emotional connection. The act of writing helps to untangle complex feelings, reveal underlying patterns, and promote a deeper understanding of ourselves and our relationships.

# Cultivating present-moment awareness for more meaningful interactions.

Offering hands-on activities to enhance relationship skills can be transformative. Mindfulness practices for better interactions provide a solid foundation. Engaging in mindfulness meditation techniques can calm the mind and improve focus, leading to more meaningful connections.

Here is what you can do to integrate mindfulness meditation into your daily life:

- Find a quiet place where you won't be disturbed.

- Sit comfortably with your back straight and close your eyes.

- Focus on your breath, taking slow, deep inhales and exhales.

- Observe your thoughts without judgment, bringing your attention back to your breath if your mind wanders.

- Practice this for 5-10 minutes each day, gradually increasing the duration as you become more comfortable.

Breathing exercises play a crucial role in regulating emotions during challenging conversations. When you feel overwhelmed or stressed, controlled breathing can help you stay grounded and respond rather than react.

To practice effective breathing exercises:

- Begin by inhaling deeply through your nose, filling your lungs completely.

- Hold your breath for a count of four.

- Exhale slowly through your mouth, allowing your body to relax with each breath out.

- Repeat this cycle several times until you feel calmer and more composed.

Mindful listening is another essential technique that enhances communication and reduces misunderstandings. By being fully present and attentive to the speaker, you demonstrate respect and empathy, fostering stronger connections.

Here are steps to practice mindful listening:

- Set aside distractions and focus entirely on the person speaking.

- Maintain eye contact and nod occasionally to show you are engaged.

- Avoid interrupting; let the speaker finish their thoughts before responding.

- Reflect back what you heard to ensure understanding, using phrases like "What I hear you saying is..."

Lastly, body scan meditation helps recognize physical cues of stress and relaxation. This awareness allows you to manage your reactions and maintain a balanced state during interactions.

To perform a body scan meditation:

- Lie down or sit comfortably, closing your eyes.

- Bring your attention to your toes and slowly move up your body, noting any areas of tension or discomfort.

- As you focus on each part, imagine sending breath and relaxation to those areas.

- Continue scanning up to the top of your head, aiming to release tension and achieve overall relaxation.

These mindfulness practices collectively enable individuals to be more present in their relationships. By reducing reactivity and increasing connection through mindful engagement, people can navigate interactions with greater calmness and clarity. Ultimately, such practices foster an environment where empathy, understanding, and genuine connection thrive, enhancing overall relationship quality.

# Strengthening communication skills through interactive exercises.

In an age of digital communication and busy schedules, hands-on activities can greatly enhance relationship skills among couples and friends. These exercises focus on improving communication, conflict resolution, nonverbal cues, and providing constructive feedback, thus creating stronger bonds and deeper connections.

Communication exercises are fundamental in fostering healthy interactions. Role-playing scenarios allow individuals to practice active listening and effective expression. Here's what you can do in order to achieve the goal:

- Begin by deciding on a topic or scenario that resonates with both participants.

- One person starts speaking about the chosen topic while the other listens attentively without interrupting.

- The listener then paraphrases what they heard to ensure they have understood correctly.

- Roles switch, giving each person the opportunity to practice both speaking and listening.

Conflict resolution simulations are equally important for learning negotiation and compromise strategies. Practicing these skills can turn potential arguments into productive discussions. Here is what you can do in order to achieve the goal:

- Choose a common conflict scenario that feels realistic.

- Designate one person as 'Person A' and the other as 'Person B.'

- 'Person A' describes their perspective on the issue while 'Person B' listens actively.

- Afterward, 'Person B' repeats back what they understood and offers their perspective.

- Both individuals work together to find a mutually beneficial resolution, emphasizing understanding and empathy.

Nonverbal communication exercises can significantly enhance understanding beyond words. Often, body language speaks volumes more than spoken words. Practicing simple exercises like mirroring each other's movements can make you aware of the subtle messages sent through gestures and facial expressions. Here is what you can do in order to achieve the goal:

- Sit facing each other in a comfortable space.

- Take turns mimicking each other's movements slowly and intentionally.

- Discuss how certain gestures and expressions make you feel and what they might convey.

Feedback sessions provide an excellent opportunity to improve communication patterns and address concerns constructively. This involves discussing recent interactions and providing honest yet compassionate feedback. Here is what you can do in order to achieve the goal:

- Set aside dedicated time for a feedback session.

- Each person takes a turn to speak about what went well in recent interactions and what could be improved.

- Focus on "I" statements to express personal feelings and avoid assigning blame.

- Offer specific examples and suggest ways to handle similar situations better in the future.

By engaging in these exercises, you will develop practical communication skills, leading to clearer exchanges, deeper empathy, and reduced misunderstandings in their relationships. When practiced regularly, these activities can transform the way individuals interact, ensuring that all parties feel heard, understood, and valued.

It's important to approach these practices with an open mind and willingness to learn. Building strong relationships requires effort, but the rewards of enhanced understanding and connection make it worthwhile. Whether you are looking to strengthen your bond with a partner or deepen your friendships, these hands-on activities provide valuable tools for navigating life's daily interactions.

## Promoting teamwork and cohesion through collaborative activities.

Offering hands-on activities to enhance relationship skills is crucial for fostering deeper connections and promoting individual growth. Through a variety of group activities, problem-solving challenges, expressive arts, and group reflections, individuals can learn to work together towards common goals, enhancing their sense of unity and shared purpose.

Group activities to foster team cohesion are foundational in building relationships. These exercises are designed to enhance trust and cooperation within any relationship. One effective way to start is through simple icebreaker activities that help participants get acquainted with each other in a fun and non-threatening manner. The familiarization process starts here, laying the groundwork for more profound connections.

From there, team-building exercises like trust falls or obstacle courses can be introduced. These activities require participants to rely on one another, thus strengthening their ability to collaborate effectively. To make these exercises successful:

- Begin with basic introductions and simple tasks.

- Gradually increase the complexity as comfort levels rise.

- Focus on activities that require mutual support and communication.

Problem-solving challenges foster shared decision making and mutual support. When individuals face challenges together, they learn to depend on each other's strengths and compensate for each other's weaknesses. For example, consider integrating activities like escape rooms or puzzle-solving sessions where participants must work collaboratively to achieve a common goal. Here's how to organize these activities:

- Present a problem that requires collective effort to solve.

- Encourage open dialogue about potential solutions.

- Celebrate the collaborative effort regardless of the outcome.

Expressive arts activities offer a unique avenue for creative expression and bonding. Whether it's through painting, music, or drama, these activities provide a space for individuals to express themselves freely and connect on an emotional level. Art can often communicate what words cannot, making it a powerful tool for building deeper relationships. To implement expressive arts activities:

- Provide art supplies and create a comfortable space for creativity.

- Encourage participants to share stories behind their creations.

- Use collaborative projects to build a sense of joint accomplishment.

Group reflections are essential in celebrating achievements and strengthening group dynamics. After a series of activities, it's vital to pause and reflect on what has been accomplished collectively. Group reflection sessions should be structured to ensure everyone has a voice and feels valued. Here's how to conduct effective group reflections:

- Create a safe environment where everyone feels comfortable sharing.

- Ask open-ended questions to prompt deeper thinking and discussion.

- Highlight both individual contributions and collective successes.

These activities underscore the importance of teamwork in achieving common goals and creating a unified group dynamic. When individuals feel connected to their peers through shared experiences, they are more likely to engage actively and support each other, which in turn reinforces the sense of community.

Understanding the importance of working together towards common goals is pivotal. It fosters a sense of unity and shared purpose, which are the cornerstones of strong relationships. When people realize that they can achieve more collectively than individually, it not only boosts morale but also reinforces the value of each member's contribution.

By participating in these group activities, individuals will develop a greater appreciation for the power of collaboration and the joy that comes from working together. Over time, these experiences help build a supportive network where trust, empathy, and mutual respect thrive. It's through these hands-on activities that individuals can truly enhance their relationship skills, creating bonds that are resilient and deeply satisfying.

Throughout this chapter, we have examined various hands-on activities designed to enhance relationship skills. From the importance of self-reflection and mindfulness meditation to engaging in role-playing scenarios and collaborative problem-solving, these tools have been presented as ways to foster deeper connections and improve communication.

Returning to our initial focus on offering hands-on activities, it's clear that these practices provide a structured method for individuals to explore their inner worlds and better understand their interactions with others. This understanding is crucial in creating more meaningful relationships.

Our current position reaffirms the value of these techniques. Journaling, mindfulness, and interactive exercises are not just casual suggestions but essential practices that contribute significantly to personal growth and relational harmony. By integrating these activities into daily routines, individuals can achieve greater emotional awareness and express themselves more authentically.

Some you might wonder about the practicality of incorporating these practices into their busy lives. The concern is valid, given the pace of modern life. However, even small acts of journaling or brief moments of mindfulness can yield substantial benefits over time. It is important to recognize that consistency, rather than duration, often leads to the most meaningful changes.

The wider implications of neglecting such activities can be significant. Lacking self-awareness and effective communication skills may lead to misunderstandings, conflicts, and strained relationships. Conversely, embracing these practices can transform interactions, fostering environments where empathy, understanding, and genuine connection thrive.

As we conclude this chapter, consider how integrating these hands-on activities can impact your relationships. Reflect on the ways you currently engage with others and how these new tools could bring deeper insight and connection. Embrace the journey of exploring these practices and discovering the profound effects they can have, both individually and collectively.

# References

*25+ Engaging Team Building Activities for Students to Foster Collaboration | Lemonade Day. lemonadeday.org.* (n.d.). https://lemonadeday.org/blog/team-building-activities-for-students.

Brinn, J. (2021, July). *Icebreakers Part 3: Building trust and creating a safe environment. MSU Extension.* https://www.canr.msu.edu/news/icebreakers_part_3_building_trust_and_creating_a_safe_environment.

Gillis Chapman, S. (2019, July). *How Mindful Communication Makes Us More Compassionate. Mindful.* https://www.mindful.org/stop-go-wait/.

*How to Strengthen Loving Relationships with Mindfulness. Mindful.* (2021, February). https://www.mindful.org/how-to-be-mindful-in-love/.

Institute, L. (2021, June). *Top Communication Exercises for Couples Revealed. Love Discovery.* https://www.lovediscovery.org/post/topcommunication-exercises-for-couples-revealed.

Schoonover, J. (n.d.). *Why Journaling Is the Best Tool for Self-Discovery | Grit and Grace Life. * https://thegritandgraceproject.org/life-and-culture/why-journaling-is-the-best-tool-for-self-discovery.

admin. (2014, November). *Journaling to Self-Discovery*. *SIYLI*. https://siyli.org/journaling/.

# Chapter Ten

# Relationships in the Digital Age

In a world where technology is ever-present, our relationships have evolved in ways that were once unimaginable. From instant messaging to social media interactions, digital communication has altered the landscape of how we connect with each other. The convenience and immediacy of these tools offer a new realm of possibilities for maintaining relationships, but they also introduce a unique set of challenges. This chapter delves into the multifaceted ways in which technology impacts modern relationships, offering insights into both its benefits and drawbacks.

One significant challenge of digital communication is the potential for misunderstandings. Unlike face-to-face conversations, digital messages often lack the non-verbal cues that are essential for conveying emotions and intentions accurately. For example, a simple joke or sarcastic comment can easily be misinterpreted when stripped of tone, facial expressions, and context. These misunderstandings can lead to conflicts and emotional disconnects, highlighting the limitations of technology in nurturing intimate connections. Moreover, the constant barrage of notifications and the pressure to remain perpetually online can create stress and detract from meaningful, real-life interactions.

This chapter will explore various aspects of digital communication's role in modern relationships. It will examine the advantages of staying connected across long distances and the ways technology can offer support in daily life. Concurrently, it will address the emotional depth that may be lost in digital exchanges and the importance of setting healthy boundaries to balance virtual and in-person interactions. By understanding these dynamics, you can better navigate their relationships in the digital age, leveraging technology to enhance connections while mitigating its potential downsides. Through a careful analysis of these issues, the chapter aims to provide practical strategies for fostering fulfilling relationships amidst the complexities of our digital world.

# Discuss the advantages and challenges of digital communication in relationships.

In today's world, technology has transformed how we communicate and engage in relationships. Digital communication offers several advantages but also brings significant challenges worth exploring.

One major benefit of digital communication is the ability to facilitate quick interactions. Messages are sent and received almost instantaneously, which makes it easier to stay connected with loved ones despite busy schedules or long distances. This rapid exchange can enhance daily coordination and provide a sense of constant support, which is crucial for maintaining strong relationships.

However, the swift nature of digital communication often lacks emotional depth. Unlike face-to-face conversations, digital messages lack non-verbal cues —such as body language, facial expressions, and tone of voice—which are critical for conveying emotions and intentions accurately. This absence can lead to misunderstandings where the true sentiment behind words is lost or misinterpreted. For instance, sarcasm or jokes may not translate well through text alone, causing unintended offense or confusion.

Despite these drawbacks, digital communication can also bridge large geographical distances, making it possible for families and friends around the world to maintain close relationships. Video calls, social media platforms, and messaging apps enable people to share experiences and milestones regardless of physical location. Yet, even with this connectivity, there is a risk that the convenience of digital interaction might hinder authentic connections. The ease and frequency of online communication can sometimes replace more meaningful in-person interactions, leading to superficial relationships that may lack depth.

Given these complexities, it's essential to establish healthy digital boundaries to maintain relationship quality. One way to achieve this is by setting limits on screen time, which helps prioritize face-to-face connections. Instead of scrolling through social media during dinner, consider putting devices away to fully engage with those around you. This practice encourages more profound and genuine interactions, fostering stronger bonds.

Additionally, sharing personal information online requires careful consideration to protect intimacy. Here are some guidelines for maintaining discretion while staying connected:

- Be mindful of the details you choose to share publicly. Avoid posting sensitive or deeply personal information that could be misused.

- Discuss with your partner or family members the types of content you are comfortable sharing about each other to respect privacy and consent.

- Create private groups or chats for more intimate conversations rather than sharing everything on public platforms.

By implementing these strategies, individuals can enjoy the benefits of digital communication while mitigating its potential drawbacks. It's important to recognize that while technology can connect us, it should complement rather than replace direct, heartfelt interactions.

In conclusion, digital communication presents both advantages and challenges in modern relationships. Quick interactions and the ability to bridge distances are significant benefits; however, the lack of emotional depth and potential for misunderstanding due to missing non-verbal cues highlight its limitations. Setting digital boundaries and being mindful of the information shared online can help preserve the quality and authenticity of relationships. As we navigate this digital age, balancing technological convenience with human connection remains key.

# Explore online etiquette guidelines and its influence on relationships.

Online Etiquette in Relationships

Understanding the importance of respectful and considerate behavior in digital interactions is crucial for maintaining and nurturing modern relationships. In a world where much of our communication happens online, it's essential to remember that our words, tone, and actions in digital spaces carry as much weight as they do face-to-face.

Here is what you can do in order to achieve the goal:

- Always be mindful of your language and tone. Digital conversations often lack context, making it easy for messages to be misinterpreted.

- Make a habit of expressing appreciation and empathy, just as you would in person.

- Take time to understand the other person's perspective before responding, which helps in avoiding unnecessary conflicts.

How courtesy and politeness online can strengthen relationships cannot be overstated. When we apply the same principles of respect and kindness that we use in face-to-face interactions, we reinforce the bonds we share with our loved ones. Simple acts like saying "please" and "thank you," acknowledging responses, and being patient in waiting for replies can go a long way in creating a positive communication environment.

Addressing the impact of tone and language in digital conversations on relationship dynamics reveals how easily misunderstandings can arise. Without facial expressions, body language, or vocal inflections, a message intended to be humorous might come off as sarcastic or offensive. Being clear, direct, and thoughtful in our digital communication helps prevent these pitfalls.

Social Media Influence

Investigating how social media platforms shape perceptions and interactions in relationships is necessary for understanding the full impact of these technologies on our lives. Social media offers opportunities to stay connected with friends and family, but it also introduces challenges that can affect our relationships negatively.

The role of social media in fostering connections but also creating jealousy and comparison is significant. On one hand, platforms like Facebook and Instagram keep us updated about loved ones' lives and help maintain distant relationships. On the other hand, they can lead to feelings of inadequacy when we compare our own lives to the curated and often idealized portrayals of others. This comparison can result in unnecessary strain and insecurity within our relationships.

Ways to mitigate negative effects of social media on self-esteem and relationship satisfaction include setting realistic expectations and recognizing the difference between online personas and real life. It's important to remind ourselves that people tend to share highlights rather than their everyday struggles.

Here are some strategies to help:

- Limit your exposure to social media if you find it affects your mood or self-perception negatively.

- Engage in conversations with your partner about any insecurities or jealousy triggered by social media.

- Focus on your own relationship's unique strengths and milestones rather than comparing them to others'.

Key takeaways: You should grasp the significance of online etiquette for nurturing healthy relationships and be mindful of the impact of social media on perceptions and behaviors.

As Alex, my approach to these topics is rooted in empirical evidence and personal experience. By applying courteous and considerate behavior online, we can nurture stronger and more resilient relationships. Being aware of how social media influences our perceptions helps us mitigate its negative impacts and focus on what truly matters: our personal connections and well-being.

# Examine the balance between virtual and face-to-face interactions in modern relationships.

Balancing Virtual and In-Person Interactions

In today's world, where technology permeates every aspect of our lives, balancing virtual and in-person interactions is essential for nurturing meaningful relationships. It's crucial to appreciate the importance of integrating both forms of communication without letting one overshadow the other.

## Prioritizing Face-to-Face Time

Face-to-face interactions are invaluable for deepening emotional connections. While digital tools offer convenience, nothing can replace the nuances of in person communication—the body language, eye contact, and physical presence that drive deeper understanding and empathy. To prioritize face-to face time:

- Spend regular, uninterrupted time together, whether it's over a meal or during a shared activity.

- Schedule routine meet-ups, even if it requires planning ahead due to busy schedules.

- Put away digital devices during these times to remain fully present with one another.

## Incorporating Digital Tools

When circumstances prevent physical meetings, incorporating digital tools can maintain and even strengthen connections. However, we must use these tools mindfully to ensure they serve as a supplement rather than a replacement for in-person interactions:

- Use video calls for a more personal touch rather than relying solely on texts or emails.

- Set specific times for digital check-ins, ensuring they're substantive and meaningful.

- Mix in creative ways of connecting online, like sharing virtual activities or playing games together.

Nurturing Relationships Across Platforms

Navigating relationships across both virtual and real world platforms requires a strategic approach to ensure growth and trust. Harmonizing these interactions begins with recognizing the strengths and limitations inherent in each form of communication.

## Building Trust Through Balanced Communication

Trust is foundational in any relationship and can be fostered through a blend of online and offline communication. Each mode offers unique opportunities for connection:

- Share important news face-to-face whenever possible to convey sincerity.

- Use digital communication for regular, casual updates, creating a steady flow of interaction.

- Be transparent about your feelings and intentions in both mediums to build a trustworthy rapport.

**Enhancing Emotional Intimacy**

Emotional intimacy thrives when there's a balance between digital and in-person engagements. Achieving this equilibrium encourages openness and vulnerability, enriching the connection:

- Prioritize frequent in-person conversations for discussing complex emotions and sensitive topics.

- Complement these with heartfelt digital messages or voice notes to stay connected between meetings.

- Plan and share future goals and dreams both online and offline to solidify emotional bonds.

Key Takeaways

Striking a healthy balance between digital and face to-face interactions is essential for sustaining and deepening relationships. By leveraging the strengths of both mediums, we can create robust connections that thrive on versatility and adaptability. Integrating virtual tools thoughtfully while prioritizing in-person engagements allows us to experience the best of both worlds, leading to richer and more fulfilling relationships.

# Investigate the impact of social media on modern relationships.

Social media platforms have undoubtedly transformed how we interact and form relationships. On one hand, these platforms allow us to stay connected with loved ones regardless of geographical distances. However, they can also introduce challenges that may affect the quality of our relationships.

Understanding how social media dynamics influence relationship dynamics is crucial. Social media often creates a curated version of one's life, which can lead to misunderstandings and unrealistic expectations. Seeing only the highlights of others' lives can cause feelings of inadequacy or jealousy. It's essential to acknowledge this curated reality and focus on open and honest communication within relationships.

Exploring the role of social media in relationship jealousy and trust issues reveals some complexities. Constantly monitoring a partner's online activities can breed insecurity and mistrust. This surveillance can lead to negative assumptions that might not be grounded in reality. It's vital to establish boundaries and communicate openly about any concerns to maintain trust.

Strategies for using social media to enhance rather than detract from relationship satisfaction are key. Here is what you can do:

- Share positive experiences and achievements to build mutual support.

- Set specific times for social media use to ensure quality time with each other.

- Avoid comparing your relationship to others by reminding yourselves that social media often showcases idealized versions of reality.

Promoting mental and emotional well-being in the digital age is essential for healthier relationships. Social media can be overwhelming and distracting, potentially leading to emotional exhaustion. To counteract this, engage in meaningful offline activities together, such as hobbies or outdoor activities, to strengthen your bond outside the digital realm.

The importance of digital detoxes cannot be overstated. Periodically disconnecting from social media allows individuals to refocus on real-world connections and be present in the moment. Spending time without digital interruptions fosters deeper conversations and enhances the quality of interactions.

Cultivating mindfulness in digital interactions can prevent relationship strains. Here is what you can do:

- Be conscious of how much time you spend on social media when with your partner.

- Practice active listening by putting away devices during important conversations.

- Reflect regularly on how digital interactions impact your emotional state and relationship health.

By managing social media effectively, couples can reduce potential negatives while enhancing their relationship satisfaction.

Recognizing the significance of managing social media influences on relationships is essential. Awareness enables individuals to take proactive steps towards fostering healthier connections. By prioritizing digital well-being and implementing thoughtful strategies, it becomes possible to navigate the complexities of modern relationships more effectively.

In conclusion, social media presents both opportunities and challenges for relationships. Understanding its influence on jealousy, trust, and overall dynamics is the first step towards leveraging it positively. Promoting digital well-being through mindfulness and periodic detoxes can safeguard relationships against potential pitfalls. With careful management, social media can indeed be a tool for enhancing, rather than detracting from, relationship satisfaction.

## Understand the multifaceted impact of technology on relationships and adopt strategies to balance digital and real-world interactions for healthier connections.

Digital communication has reshaped the landscape of modern relationships, bringing both advantages and challenges to how we connect with others. We've explored the benefits of quick interactions and the ability to bridge vast distances, enabling us to maintain connections with loved ones despite geographical separations. However, these conveniences come with their own set of drawbacks, such as the lack of emotional depth in digital exchanges and the potential for misunderstandings due to the absence of non-verbal cues.

Our initial discussion highlighted the transformative power of technology in keeping us connected. Yet, as we've delved deeper, it's become clear that there are significant concerns regarding the quality and authenticity of these interactions. The ease of digital communication can sometimes replace more meaningful face-to-face engagements, leading to superficial connections that may not provide the emotional support we truly need.

It's essential to acknowledge the implications of these findings. While quick messages and video calls can help maintain relationships, they should not be a substitute for in-person communication. The lack of physical presence and non-verbal cues can lead to misinterpretations and weaken the emotional bonds that hold relationships together. Additionally, the convenience of staying connected online can sometimes make us complacent, reducing the effort we put into nurturing our relationships through more meaningful interactions.

Looking ahead, you should be mindful of the potential consequences of over-relying on digital communication. In a broader context, an excessive lean on technology could contribute to a society where superficial connections become the norm, undermining the depth and richness of human relationships. This shift could impact our overall well-being, as genuine social connections are crucial for emotional and psychological health.

As we navigate this digital age, it's important to strike a balance between virtual and face-to-face interactions. Setting digital boundaries, prioritizing face-to-face time, and being mindful of what we share online will help preserve the quality of our relationships. Embracing the strengths of both digital and in-person communication will lead to richer, more fulfilling connections. Ultimately, the key lies in using technology to complement, rather than replace, the deep and heartfelt interactions that form the foundation of strong, lasting relationships.

# References


*Advantages and Disadvantages of Digital Signals. GeeksforGeeks.* (2020, December). https://www.geeksforgeeks.org/advantages-anddisadvantages-of-digital-signals/.

Anderson, M., Vogels, E. (2020, May). *Dating and Relationships in the Digital Age. Pew Research Center: Internet, Science & Tech.* https://

www.pewresearch.org/internet/2020/05/08/datinga
nd-relationships-in-the-digital-age/.


*Balance between digital and face-to-face friends |
Student Health and Wellness | Liberty University.
Student Health and Wellness.* (2021, October).
https://www.liberty.edu/students/health-wellness/
becoming-wellness-champions-blog/balancebetween-
digital-and-face-to-face-interactions/.


Barbosa, B., Galvan Vela, E., Herzallah, A., Liu, F.,
Ostic, D., Qalati, S., Shah, S. (2021, June). *Effects of
Social Media Use on Psychological Well-Being: A
Mediated Model. Frontiers in Psychology.* https://
www.frontiersin.org/articles/10.3389/fpsyg.
2021.678766/full.


National University. (2017, May). *The Dangers of
Social Media on Marriage and Family. National
University.* https://www.nu.edu/blog/the-dangersof-
social-media-on-marriage-and-family/.

# Chapter Eleven

# Creating Conscious Relationships

Relationships are the cornerstone of our lives, shaping our experiences and providing a sense of belonging. However, many relationships fall short of their potential due to a lack of conscious engagement and awareness. Imagine if every interaction you had with your partner, friends, or family was filled with presence and intention. What would it mean for the quality of your connections? This chapter explores how integrating conscious awareness can transform the way we relate to one another, leading to deeper, more fulfilling bonds.

At the heart of relationship challenges lies a common problem: the absence of mindfulness in our interactions. Often, individuals engage in conversations without truly listening, distracted by their thoughts or external stimuli. For instance, consider a scenario where a couple argues because one partner feels unheard while the other plans a response instead of genuinely listening. This lack of presence creates barriers to understanding and empathy, making it difficult to address underlying issues. When we fail to be fully present, our relationships become superficial, lacking the depth required for genuine connection.

In this chapter, we will delve into the concept of conscious relationships and how they elevate the quality of our connections. We will explore the impact of being fully present during interactions and provide actionable steps to foster genuine listening and empathetic responses. The chapter will also highlight the benefits of mindfulness, such as enhanced emotional regulation and reduced reactivity in conflicts. Additionally, we will discuss how mindful practices promote authenticity and vulnerability, essential elements for building trust and intimacy. By understanding and applying these principles, you can cultivate healthier, more resilient relationships that stand the test of time.

# Understanding the concept of conscious relationships and how it elevates the quality of connections.

Integrating conscious awareness to build and sustain healthier relationships begins with the concept of conscious relationships. This involves being fully present and mindful in all interactions, fostering deeper understanding and connection. When we are fully present, we engage in genuine listening and empathetic responses, creating an environment where authenticity and vulnerability can thrive. Conscious relationships lead to more meaningful and fulfilling connections, allowing us to truly understand and appreciate the people around us.

Being fully present allows for genuine listening and empathetic responses. Here is what you can do to achieve this:

- Pay close attention during conversations without planning your response while the other person is talking.

- Make eye contact and use body language that shows you are engaged and interested.

- Reflect back what you've heard to ensure understanding and show empathy.

- Avoid interrupting or diverting the conversation back to yourself immediately.

Mindfulness in relationships promotes authenticity and vulnerability, essential elements for any deep connection. When we practice mindfulness, we become more attuned to our partner's needs and feelings, creating a safe space for open communication. In turn, this paves the way for us to be vulnerable and authentic, knowing we are seen and valued for who we truly are. Cultivating these conscious relationships helps combat superficial interactions and fosters trust and intimacy.

Benefits of practicing mindfulness in relationships are profound. Mindfulness enhances emotional regulation and empathy (Hu et al., 2022). It reduces reactivity in conflicts, promoting constructive resolutions. By being aware of our internal states, we can respond rather than react, leading to healthier discussions and problem-solving dynamics. Here is what you can do to reduce reactivity in conflicts:

- Take deep breaths before responding in a heated moment.
- Pause and think about the best course of action during disagreements.
- Communicate your feelings calmly and clearly.
- Focus on resolving the issue rather than winning the argument.

Enhanced self-awareness through mindfulness deepens understanding of personal triggers and reactions. Understanding what sets off certain emotions allows us to step back and choose how to act, rather than simply reacting out of habit or impulse. Here is what you can do to enhance self-awareness:

- Keep a journal to reflect on your thoughts and feelings daily.

- Practice meditation regularly to become familiar with your mental patterns.

- Seek feedback from trusted friends or family members on your behavior.

- Observe your emotional reactions and question their root causes.

Practicing mindfulness fosters greater compassion and empathy towards others. By being present and aware, we can better put ourselves in others' shoes, leading to more empathetic interactions and a richer emotional life. Here is what you can do to foster empathy:

- Actively listen to others and try to understand their perspective.

- Engage in activities that encourage compassion, such as volunteering.

- Practice self-compassion to extend that kindness to others naturally.

- Educate yourself about different cultures and experiences to broaden your understanding.

The benefits of practicing mindfulness in relationships cannot be overstated. Mindfulness not only enhances emotional regulation but also promotes empathy, helping us connect on a deeper level. By practicing mindfulness, we increase our ability to handle conflicts constructively and foster more compassionate interactions. Mindful communication reduces misunderstandings, increases mutual respect, and creates a foundation for long-lasting fulfillment in our relationships.

Incorporating conscious awareness into our relationships takes effort, but the rewards are worth it. Being present and mindful transforms our interactions, making them more meaningful and enriching. Mindfulness offers valuable tools for managing our emotions, understanding ourselves and others better, and maintaining healthy, loving connections. Practicing mindfulness is a journey toward greater emotional intelligence and stronger relationships built on understanding, empathy, and respect.

True fulfillment in relationships comes from this depth of connection and understanding, which mindfulness facilitates beautifully. When we bring conscious awareness to our interactions, we pave the way for a richer, more rewarding relational experience. Whether navigating through life's challenges or celebrating its joys, a mindful approach ensures that our relationships remain strong and supportive, providing a solid foundation for growth and happiness.

# Exploring the benefits of daily rituals in maintaining connection and intimacy.

Implementing daily rituals to stay connected is a cornerstone for building and sustaining healthier relationships. Establishing routines that nurture the relationship bond creates a sense of stability and continuity. Here's how you can do this effectively:

- Start with simple yet meaningful daily check-ins. Set aside time each day, even if it's just for a few minutes, to talk about your day, share your thoughts, and listen actively to your partner. This promotes open communication and shared experiences, creating a safe space where both partners feel heard and valued.

- Mealtime conversations are another powerful ritual. Whether it's breakfast, lunch, or dinner, use this time to engage in meaningful dialogues. Discuss your plans for the day, share what you're grateful for, or simply enjoy each other's company without distractions.

- Bedtime reflections can deepen emotional connections. Before sleeping, spend a few moments reflecting on the positives of the day, expressing appreciation for each other, and setting intentions for the next day. This practice not only fosters a peaceful end to the day but also strengthens the bond between partners.

Consistent practices like these build trust and intimacy over time. When routines are established with intention and care, they become symbols of your commitment to each other. The predictability and regularity of these rituals provide reassurance and stability, which are crucial for long-term relationship growth.

Long-term strategies for sustained relationship growth involve examining ways to sustain and evolve the relationship. To achieve this, invest in shared goals and aspirations. Collaborate on projects you're both passionate about, plan trips together, or set mutual financial goals. Working towards common objectives strengthens your partnership and provides a shared sense of accomplishment.

Prioritizing quality time together is essential. In our busy lives, it's easy to let quality time slip away. Dedicate uninterrupted time to engage in activities both partners enjoy, whether it's a hobby, a sport, or simply unwinding at home. Regularly scheduled "date nights" can rekindle romance and keep the connection alive.

Adapting and adjusting rituals as the relationship evolves ensures continued intimacy. As life circumstances change, be flexible with your rituals.

197

What was once a daily morning coffee might transform into a weekly brunch date as schedules shift. Being adaptable shows that you value the ritual itself and the intention behind it, rather than the specific form it takes.

Understanding the importance of daily rituals in maintaining connection is key. By establishing lasting practices for sustained growth, couples can thrive together.

Key takeaways:

1. Daily rituals like check-ins, mealtime conversations, and bedtime reflections enhance connectivity and intimacy.

2. Consistency in these practices builds trust and reassures partners of their commitment.

3. Investing in shared goals and prioritizing quality time fosters long-term growth.

4. Adaptability in rituals ensures they remain relevant and meaningful as the relationship evolves.

By integrating conscious awareness and deliberately nurturing these connections, couples can build resilient, fulfilling relationships that stand the test of time.

# Delving into the concept of conscious awareness in resolving conflicts and fostering understanding.

Practicing mindfulness in conflict resolution is about applying conscious awareness to navigate disagreements constructively. It involves being present at the moment, observing your thoughts and emotions without judgment, and responding rather than reacting impulsively.

- Stay aware of your own feelings and triggers during a disagreement.

- Focus on observing rather than immediately responding.

- Take deep breaths to center yourself and maintain calmness.

- Engage in active listening, ensuring you fully understand the other person's perspective before responding.

- Practice non-reactivity; let go of the need to defend or retaliate immediately.

Mindful communication reduces misunderstandings and promotes active listening. When we communicate mindfully, we are fully present, and this presence allows us to listen more effectively and respond with empathy and clarity.

- Pay close attention to the speaker without planning your response while they're talking.

- Reflect back what you've heard to ensure understanding.

- Use gentle, non-confrontational language to express your viewpoint.

- Avoid interrupting and give space for the other person to share fully.

Cultivating empathy during conflicts enhances mutual understanding and validation. Empathy allows us to step into another's shoes and see things from their perspective, which can bridge the gap between differing viewpoints.

- Acknowledge and validate the other person's feelings and experiences.

- Express understanding even if you don't agree with their point of view.

- Share your feelings honestly but calmly, focusing on your own experiences rather than assigning blame.

- Look for common ground where both parties' needs can be met.

Mindfulness fosters emotional regulation, preventing escalation of disagreements. By staying mindful, individuals can manage their emotions better, reducing the likelihood of conflicts escalating into full-blown arguments.

- Notice early signs of stress or anger within yourself.

- Pause and take deep breaths to calm your nervous system.

- Suggest taking a short break if emotions start to run high, then return to the conversation once calmer.

- Maintain an open and receptive posture to show you're willing to listen.

Promoting understanding through conscious interactions helps create deeper emotional connections. Conscious interactions require you to be fully present and engaged, encouraging open dialogue and fostering trust and empathy.

- Recognize and validate the emotions that arise during conflicts.

- Make it a safe space for sharing by being nonjudgmental and supportive.

- Approach each interaction with curiosity rather than criticism.

- Encourage open-ended questions to explore deeper feelings and thoughts.

Acknowledging and validating emotions during conflicts promotes empathy and helps address underlying issues.

- Actively listen to identify not just the words but the emotions behind them.

- Repeat back the feelings you perceive, such as "It sounds like you're feeling frustrated."

- Show genuine concern and interest in their wellbeing.

- Validate their emotions by affirming that it's okay to feel the way they do.

Creating a safe space for open dialogue fosters understanding and resolution. When people feel safe to express themselves without fear of judgment or retribution, they are more likely to communicate openly and honestly.

- Set clear ground rules that emphasize respect and no interruptions.

- Agree on a code word or signal to pause the discussion if it becomes too heated.

- Ensure privacy and minimize distractions during these conversations.

- Approach each discussion with a problem-solving mindset instead of a win-lose attitude.

Embracing vulnerability and authenticity strengthens the relationship bond. Being vulnerable means sharing your true feelings and experiences, even when it's uncomfortable, which fosters deeper connections and trust.

Key takeaways: Mindfulness during conflicts provides the tools to maintain composure and engage in constructive dialogue. It emphasizes the importance of empathy in resolving disputes and highlights how conscious interactions can deepen emotional connections. Through these practices, individuals can foster healthier, more resilient relationships built on understanding, support, and genuine connection.

# Highlighting the long-term benefits of integrating conscious awareness into relationship dynamics.

Building sustained connection through conscious awareness: How conscious relationships lead to lasting fulfillment

In today's fast-paced world, building and sustaining meaningful relationships requires intentional effort

203

and the presence of mind. Conscious awareness in relationships means being fully present with your partner, friends, or family and making a deliberate choice to engage thoughtfully in each interaction. This approach leads to deeper connections and long-lasting fulfillment because it emphasizes understanding, empathy, and mutual growth.

Creating a culture of appreciation and gratitude sustains positivity in the relationship. Practicing gratitude regularly can transform the dynamic between partners, friends, or family members. Here is what you can do to cultivate appreciation and gratitude:

- Make a habit of expressing thanks for both big and small gestures.

- Celebrate each other's achievements and milestones, no matter how minor they may seem.

- Create rituals such as daily affirmations or weekly gratitude circles to reinforce positive interactions.

- Keep a shared gratitude journal where both parties can contribute their thoughts and acknowledgments.

Applying mindfulness in everyday interactions deepens intimacy and understanding. Mindfulness encourages individuals to focus on the present moment without judgment. By integrating mindfulness into daily interactions, you can foster stronger bonds. Here are some steps to help you apply mindfulness:

- Practice active listening by really focusing on what the other person is saying without planning your response while they speak.

- Pay attention to non-verbal cues such as body language and facial expressions.

- Take a few deep breaths before responding to emotionally charged situations to maintain calmness and clarity.

- Engage in shared mindfulness exercises like meditation or mindful walks together.

Prioritizing conscious connections fosters a strong foundation for long-term growth. When individuals make an effort to nurture their relationships consciously, they create an environment that supports mutual respect, trust, and affection. This foundation helps couples, friends, and families weather life's challenges together, leading to a more resilient and fulfilling relationship.

Nurturing relationship growth through conscious practices: The role of conscious awareness in evolving relationships

As relationships develop and evolve, maintaining conscious awareness ensures that both parties grow together rather than apart. Embracing personal growth and self-awareness enhances the partnership's development. By continuously working on themselves and their habits, individuals contribute positively to the health of their relationships. Growth is not just about changing for the better but also about understanding oneself deeply and aligning one's actions with core values.

Consistent practice of mindfulness and conscious communication nurtures ongoing connection. Clear and honest communication is key to any healthy relationship. By practicing conscious communication, you can avoid misunderstandings and build a deeper connection. Here are guidelines on how to implement this practice:

- Set aside regular time for open and honest conversations without distractions.

- Use "I" statements to express feelings and concerns, which reduces defensiveness.

- Validate each other's experiences even if you disagree, showing empathy and support.

- Be willing to apologize and forgive when necessary, understanding that mistakes are part of growth.

Celebrating milestones and shared successes reinforces the bond and commitment. Taking the time to honor significant moments and achievements strengthens the emotional connection between partners. This practice can range from celebrating anniversaries and birthdays to acknowledging personal accomplishments and shared goals. Here's how you can celebrate together:

- Plan special outings or activities that both enjoy to commemorate important dates.

- Share your successes openly and take pride in each other's achievements.

- Create shared goals and celebrate when you reach them, reinforcing teamwork.

- Reflect on your journey together during these celebrations to appreciate how far you've come.

By integrating these conscious practices into your relationships, you can nurture sustained connection and ensure long-term fulfillment. Conscious awareness allows for genuine, heartfelt interactions that ground the relationship in mutual respect, understanding, and continual growth. As you apply these principles, you'll find that your relationships are not just surviving but thriving, serving as a source of strength and joy in your life.

# Key takeaways

In this chapter, we explored how integrating conscious awareness into our interactions can build and sustain healthier relationships. We began by understanding the concept of conscious relationships and how being fully present in our interactions can lead to deeper connections. Through mindfulness and genuine engagement, we were able to foster environments where authenticity and vulnerability thrive, resulting in more meaningful and fulfilling connections.

Reflecting on this, it's clear that being mindful requires effort but significantly impacts the quality of our relationships. By practicing techniques such as active listening and empathetic responding, we create a safe space for open communication. This approach promotes trust and intimacy, essential elements for any relationship.

We also discussed specific strategies to enhance mindfulness in everyday interactions, such as paying close attention during conversations and using body language that shows engagement. These simple yet effective methods help develop emotional regulation and reduce conflict reactivity. In turn, this enables us to navigate disagreements constructively, promoting healthier discussions and problem-solving dynamics.

An important point raised was the need for consistency and adaptability in our conscious practices. Establishing daily rituals, like check-ins and bedtime reflections, creates stability and continuity in our relationships. However, life evolves, and so should our routines. Flexibility in these practices ensures they remain relevant and meaningful, fostering long-term relationship growth.

Moreover, the profound benefits of mindfulness extend beyond improved emotional regulation. By enhancing self-awareness, we better understand our triggers and reactions, allowing us to respond rather than react impulsively. This awareness not only helps manage our emotions but also fosters greater compassion and empathy towards others.

As we conclude this chapter, consider the wider consequences of integrating conscious awareness into your relationships. It cultivates a culture of appreciation and gratitude, transforming relationship dynamics positively. Whether with partners, friends, or family, adopting these principles can lead to resilient, fulfilling connections that stand the test of time.

Ultimately, the journey toward mindful relationships is ongoing, requiring continuous effort and reflection. But the rewards—a richer, more rewarding relational experience—are worth it. Embrace this mindful approach, and you'll find your relationships strengthening, providing a solid foundation for growth and happiness.

# References

Assi, M., Eshah, N., Rayan, A. (2022, January). *The Relationship Between Mindfulness and Conflict Resolution Styles Among Nurse Managers: A CrossSectional Study. SAGE Open Nursing.* None.

Gazder, T., Stanton, S. (2020, October). *Partners' Relationship Mindfulness Promotes Better Daily Relationship Behaviours for Insecurely Attached Individuals. International Journal of Environmental Research and Public Health.* None.

*How to Create Daily Intimacy Rituals. Couple Summit.* (n.d.). https://www.thecouplesummit.org/blog/Intimacy-rituals.

Hu, Z., Lin, Y., Lin, Y., Shi, J., Wang, Y., Wang, Y., Wen, Y., Yu, Z. (2022, October). *Effectiveness of mindfulness-based interventions on empathy: A meta-analysis. Frontiers in Psychology.* None.

Lip, M., Mandal, E. (2021). *Mindfulness, relationship quality, and conflict

*Rituals Strengthen Couples. Here's Why They're Good for Business, Too. HBS Working Knowledge.* (2019, June).
https://hbswk.hbs.edu/item/ritualsstrengthen-couples-here-s-why-they-re-good-forbusiness-too.

Weir, K. (2018, March). *Life-saving relationships. [https://www.apa.org.* ](https://www.apa.org.*) https://www.apa.org/monitor/2018/03/life-savingrelationships.

in close relationships. Current Issues in Personality Psychology.* None.

resolution strategies used by partners

Chapter Twelve

# **Reflect on the Journey**

Human relationships are deeply complex and inherently valuable. As we navigate our daily lives, we encounter individuals from diverse backgrounds and cultures, each bringing unique experiences and perspectives into our interactions. This diversity enriches our connections and contributes to the intricate tapestry of human experience. Whether through scientific research, historical anecdotes, or personal stories, examining these varied lenses can offer profound insights into the nature of our bonds with others.

However, building and maintaining such relationships presents its own set of challenges. One significant hurdle is the need for effective communication. Misunderstandings often arise from differences in cultural norms, personal biases, and even the simple nuances of language. For instance, a gesture or phrase considered polite in one culture may be perceived as rude in another. Emotional intelligence also plays a crucial role, requiring us to understand not only our emotions but also those of others. Conflicts are inevitable, but how we address them—whether through empathy and active listening or avoidance and confrontation—can significantly impact the longevity and quality of our connections.

In this chapter, we will delve into the multifaceted exploration of building relationships with a diverse range of people. We will uncover the intricacies of human connection by looking at it through scientific, historical, and personal lenses. Topics such as the importance of trust, the influence of cultural backgrounds, and the balance between online and offline interactions will be explored. By understanding these variables, you will gain practical insights and strategies to foster stronger, more meaningful relationships in their personal and professional lives.

# Emphasize Key Takeaways

As we draw from the insights gathered throughout this book, it's clear that building meaningful relationships requires a multifaceted approach. At the heart of every strong connection lies effective communication. It's more than just exchanging words; it's about genuinely understanding and responding to the needs and emotions of others. This involves active listening, where one truly hears what the other person is saying, reflecting on their words, and responding thoughtfully. Communication paves the way for

213

empathy, the ability to perceive and share the feelings of another. It's through empathy that trust begins to flourish.

Trust is the bedrock of any relationship—it cannot be demanded but must be earned over time with consistency and honesty. When individuals trust each other, they feel secure enough to open up and share their true selves without fear of judgment or ridicule. Respect follows naturally when trust is established. Respecting differences and valuing them fosters an environment where everyone feels valued and appreciated.

Recognizing cultural influences showcases our commitment to respecting diversity. Each culture brings unique perspectives, values, and traditions that enrich our interactions. By being culturally aware, we not only honor those differences but also expand our own horizons, making our relationships deeper and more meaningful.

Physical presence is important, but in today's digital age, connecting online has become a significant part of maintaining relationships. Digital dynamics introduce both opportunities and challenges. We must be mindful of the ways digital communication can sometimes lack the nuances of face-to-face interactions. Embracing the strengths of digital platforms while also being cautious of their limitations helps us maintain genuine connections.

Emotional intelligence plays a pivotal role in navigating complex relationships. It involves the ability to understand and manage one's emotions, as well as recognizing and influencing the emotions of others. A high level of emotional intelligence enhances our interpersonal relationships by allowing us to interact with empathy and sensitivity. It's crucial for resolving conflicts and ensuring that all parties feel heard and respected.

Empathy and emotional intelligence are intertwined, creating a feedback loop that strengthens our bonds with others. When we empathize, we're better equipped to respond in emotionally intelligent ways, which in turn, nurtures trust and respect further.

Practical exercises offer tangible means to enhance these qualities. Engaging in activities that promote team-building, problem-solving, and conflict resolution can significantly improve how we relate to those around us. These exercises help us practice skills in a controlled setting, making it easier to implement them in real-life scenarios.

Conscious awareness is key to sustaining healthy relationships. It involves being present and fully engaging with those around us. When we are consciously aware, we're more likely to notice the subtle cues and signals that indicate how others are feeling. This awareness allows us to react appropriately and with consideration, fostering a nurturing environment.

In summation, an insightful exploration of human connection reveals that relationships thrive when built on a foundation of effective communication, empathy, trust, and respect. Cultural influences enrich our connections, providing broader perspectives and deeper understanding. Practical exercises serve as tools for improvement, while digital dynamics offer both convenience and complexity. Conscious awareness ensures that we remain attuned to the needs and emotions of others, allowing our relationships to grow stronger and more meaningful.

Remember, effective communication lays the groundwork for meaningful connections, while empathy and trust serve as pillars of support. By embracing cultural differences, engaging in practical exercises, and nurturing conscious awareness, we can continue to strengthen and sustain our relationships. Through these practices, we not only build better relationships but also contribute to a more connected and empathetic world.

## Encourage Ongoing Growth

As we reflect on building relationships with a diverse range of people, it's important to carry forward the insights we've uncovered and continue our personal growth beyond the covers of this book. This journey is not about reaching an endpoint but about evolving continuously, adapting, and learning from every interaction.

Building meaningful connections starts with active listening. It's more than just hearing words—it's about being fully present, understanding not only what is said but also what is unspoken. Body language, tone, and emotion play a significant role in how messages are conveyed and received. To practice active listening, give your full attention to the person speaking, refrain from interrupting, and reflect back what you've heard to ensure understanding.

Emotional intelligence is another cornerstone of strong relationships. It involves recognizing, understanding, and managing our own emotions while also being attuned to the emotions of others. By developing emotional intelligence, we can respond more empathetically and constructively in our interactions. Here are practical ways you can enhance your emotional intelligence:

- Tune into your own feelings and consider what they might be telling you.

- Observe how your emotions affect your thoughts and behaviors.

- Practice empathy by putting yourself in others' shoes and seeing situations from their perspective.

- Apply these insights to manage your interactions more effectively, maintaining healthy emotional boundaries.

Engaging in regular reflection helps us learn from past experiences. Take time to ponder over your conversations and interactions. Reflecting on what went well and what didn't offers invaluable lessons for future encounters. Keep a journal where you note significant interactions, your feelings, and the outcomes. This way, you can track your development and identify patterns that need adjusting.

Human connections are often complex due to cultural influences. Our backgrounds shape our values, beliefs, and communication styles. Understanding and respecting these differences enriches our relationships. Pay attention to cultural cues and be open-minded. Ask questions and show genuine interest in learning about the traditions and viewpoints of others. This creates a bridge of understanding and mutual respect.

Practical exercises can also fortify our relationship building skills. Role-playing scenarios where you practice conflict resolution or expressing gratitude can be immensely helpful. Whether with a partner, family member, or friend, such exercises foster better communication and understanding. Engage regularly in activities together that promote teamwork and open dialogue, such as collaborative projects, games, or discussions on various topics.

In today's digital age, navigating relationships also means considering how digital dynamics influence our interactions. Social media and messaging apps create new avenues for connection but can sometimes hinder deep, face-to-face engagement. Strive for a balance between online and offline interactions. Use technology to stay connected, but prioritize in-person meetings when possible. Be mindful of digital communication etiquette, ensuring that your messages convey warmth and clarity.

A mindset of continual learning and improvement is vital. Relationships are ever-evolving, and so should our approaches to nurturing them. Attend workshops, read widely, and seek feedback from those around you. Continuous education broadens our perspectives and equips us with fresh insights to apply in our interactions.

Remember, building profound connections isn't just about personal gains. It involves social responsibility —considering the broader impact of our interactions. Contribute positively to the lives of others, offer support, and build networks that foster community well-being. This collective effort enhances not only individual relationships but society as a whole.

As we conclude, let this not be the end but rather a new beginning in your quest for deeper, more fulfilling relationships. Commit to practicing active listening, cultivating emotional intelligence, and reflecting on your interactions regularly. Embrace cultural diversity, engage in practical exercises, and navigate digital dynamics thoughtfully. By doing so, you're not just enhancing personal connections; you're contributing to a more compassionate and understanding world.

May your journey be filled with continuous growth, enriched by the connections you build, and anchored in the wisdom that relationships are not static—they are dynamic, intricate, and profoundly rewarding.

## Express Gratitude

I extend my heartfelt gratitude to you, dear you, for embarking on this journey with me. Your dedication to understanding and enhancing your relationships is a testament to your courage and commitment to personal growth. May you continue to navigate the intricacies of human connection with newfound wisdom and compassion.

Understanding human relationships is a complex endeavor. We interact with people from diverse backgrounds, cultures, and walks of life, bringing different experiences and perspectives into our exchanges. By exploring these differences through scientific, historical, and personal lenses, we can gain a deeper appreciation for the richness they bring to our lives.

From a scientific perspective, human connections are deeply rooted in our biology. Our brains are wired to seek social interaction, and neurotransmitters like oxytocin play a significant role in how we bond with others. Historical examples show that civilizations have thrived or faltered based on the strength of their social networks. Personal anecdotes remind us of the impact meaningful relationships have on our wellbeing and happiness.

Building relationships with a diverse range of people requires openness and empathy. It's important to actively listen and be genuinely curious about others' stories. Recognizing and challenging our biases helps us approach each interaction with a fresh perspective. When we take the time to understand where someone is coming from, we build a foundation of trust and mutual respect.

Connections are also shaped by the context in which they occur. The family environment, workplace dynamics, and cultural settings all influence how

221

relationships develop. Being aware of these factors allows us to navigate them more effectively. For instance, understanding cultural norms can prevent misunderstandings and foster better communication.

Balancing individual freedom with social responsibility is key to nurturing healthy relationships. While it's essential to express our own needs and desires, we must also consider the impact of our actions on others. This balance creates a dynamic where both parties feel valued and respected.

Conflict is inevitable in any relationship, but it's how we handle it that determines its outcome. Approaching disagreements with a problem-solving mindset rather than an adversarial one leads to constructive resolutions. Effective communication and emotional regulation are crucial skills in managing conflicts and maintaining strong connections.

Our interactions are further influenced by societal structures and policies. Governments and corporations play a role in shaping the environments in which relationships form. Advocacy for checks and balances ensures that these institutions work in the public's best interest, promoting a society where everyone has the opportunity to thrive.

Data and research provide valuable insights into the dynamics of human relationships. Evidence-based approaches help us identify what works and what doesn't, allowing us to make informed decisions. By staying updated on the latest findings, we can continually refine our strategies for building and maintaining connections.

Your journey towards personal growth and relationship development doesn't end here. Continuously apply the insights gained from this exploration to your everyday interactions. Here are some practical ways to do that:

- Engage in active listening during conversations

- Reflect on your own biases and challenge them

- Practice empathy by putting yourself in others' shoes

- Foster an environment of trust and respect in your relationships

By doing so, you will not only improve your own connections but also contribute to the overall wellbeing of those around you.

In conclusion, understanding and building relationships with a diverse range of people is a multifaceted endeavor. It involves considering biological, historical, and personal perspectives, while balancing individual freedom with social responsibility. By applying evidence-based insights and fostering empathy and respect, we can navigate the complexities of human connections with grace and wisdom. I'm grateful for your commitment to this journey and excited for the positive impact your efforts will have on your relationships and beyond.

## Reflect on the Journey

Throughout this chapter, we have explored the multifaceted nature of building meaningful relationships with a diverse range of people. We delved into the importance of effective communication, empathy, and trust, each serving as pillars of strong connections. By actively listening, we not only hear but also understand and respond to the needs of others, fostering deep bonds.

Trust, earned through consistency and honesty, creates a secure environment where individuals feel free to be their true selves. Respect naturally follows when trust is established, allowing us to value differences and enrich our interactions. Cultural awareness further enhances our relationships by expanding our horizons and making our connections more meaningful.

In today's digital age, maintaining relationships involves navigating both the opportunities and challenges posed by online interactions. While digital communication offers convenience, it requires mindfulness to preserve the nuances present in face to-face engagements. Balancing these dynamics ensures that our connections remain genuine and strong.

Emotional intelligence is crucial in managing one's own emotions and understanding those of others. This skill enables us to interact with empathy and sensitivity, resolving conflicts constructively and ensuring everyone feels heard and respected. Practical exercises in team-building and conflict resolution can help us hone these skills, making them easier to apply in real-life scenarios.

Conscious awareness plays a pivotal role in sustaining healthy relationships. Being fully present allows us to notice subtle cues in interactions, helping us react thoughtfully and with consideration. This heightened awareness nurtures our bonds, allowing them to grow stronger and more meaningful over time.

Reflecting on our journey reveals that relationships are dynamic and require ongoing effort. Effective communication, empathy, trust, and respect form the foundation of meaningful connections. Cultural influences, practical exercises, and digital dynamics all contribute to the complexity of human interactions. Conscious awareness ensures we stay attuned to others' needs and emotions.

As we continue on this path, it's essential to embrace personal growth, continuously applying the insights we've gained. Active listening, emotional intelligence, and reflection are key practices in nurturing our relationships. Embracing cultural diversity and balancing online with offline interactions will further enhance our connections. Through these efforts, we contribute to a more compassionate and understanding world.

Our journey doesn't end here; it's an ongoing evolution. Commit to these practices, and may your relationships flourish, enriched by the wisdom and compassion gained from this exploration. Thank you for dedicating yourself to this journey of building deeper, more fulfilling relationships.